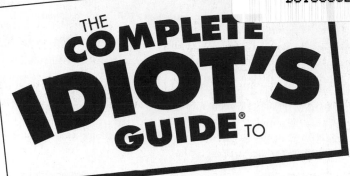

THE
COMPLETE
IDIOT'S
GUIDE® TO

The Right Words for Any Occasion

by Veronica Deisler and Marylou Ambrose

ALPHA

A member of Penguin Group (USA) Inc.

ALPHA BOOKS

Published by the Penguin Group

Penguin Group (USA) Inc., 375 Hudson Street, New York, New York 10014, USA

Penguin Group (Canada), 90 Eglinton Avenue East, Suite 700, Toronto, Ontario M4P 2Y3, Canada (a division of Pearson Penguin Canada Inc.)

Penguin Books Ltd., 80 Strand, London WC2R 0RL, England

Penguin Ireland, 25 St. Stephen's Green, Dublin 2, Ireland (a division of Penguin Books Ltd.)

Penguin Group (Australia), 250 Camberwell Road, Camberwell, Victoria 3124, Australia (a division of Pearson Australia Group Pty. Ltd.)

Penguin Books India Pvt. Ltd., 11 Community Centre, Panchsheel Park, New Delhi—110 017, India

Penguin Group (NZ), 67 Apollo Drive, Rosedale, North Shore, Auckland 1311, New Zealand (a division of Pearson New Zealand Ltd.)

Penguin Books (South Africa) (Pty.) Ltd., 24 Sturdee Avenue, Rosebank, Johannesburg 2196, South Africa

Penguin Books Ltd., Registered Offices: 80 Strand, London WC2R 0RL, England

International Standard Book Number: 978-1-59257-732-3
Library of Congress Catalog Card Number: 2007935865

10 09 08   8 7 6 5 4 3 2 1

Interpretation of the printing code: The rightmost number of the first series of numbers is the year of the book's printing; the rightmost number of the second series of numbers is the number of the book's printing. For example, a printing code of 08-1 shows that the first printing occurred in 2008.

Printed in the United States of America

Note: This publication contains the opinions and ideas of its authors. It is intended to provide helpful and informative material on the subject matter covered. It is sold with the understanding that the authors and publisher are not engaged in rendering professional services in the book. If the reader requires personal assistance or advice, a competent professional should be consulted.

The authors and publisher specifically disclaim any responsibility for any liability, loss, or risk, personal or otherwise, which is incurred as a consequence, directly or indirectly, of the use and application of any of the contents of this book.

Most Alpha books are available at special quantity discounts for bulk purchases for sales promotions, premiums, fund-raising, or educational use. Special books, or book excerpts, can also be created to fit specific needs.

For details, write: Special Markets, Alpha Books, 375 Hudson Street, New York, NY 10014.

Publisher: *Marie Butler-Knight*
Editorial Director: *Mike Sanders*
Managing Editor: *Billy Fields*
Senior Acquisitions Editor: *Paul Dinas*
Senior Development Editor: *Christy Wagner*
Production Editor: *Kayla Dugger*

Copy Editor: *Mike Dietsch*
Book Designers: *Trina Wurst/Kurt Owens*
Cover Designer: *Kurt Owens*
Indexer: *Johnna Vanhoose Dinse*
Layout: *Brian Massey*
Proofreader: *Aaron Black*

Contents at a Glance

Contents

Appendixes

Introduction

At one time, letter writing was considered an art. It was also a necessity, being the only form of long-distance communication. People used flowery language and wrote in elaborate cursive on thick vellum paper. Artists like the sixteenth-century Dutch painter Vermeer even painted portraits of people reading and writing letters.

Then along came the telephone, and that changed everything.

It took a while, but by the last quarter of the twentieth century, few people were actually writing letters anymore. And why bother, when you could "reach out and touch someone" by phone, as the AT&T slogan urged? Add to that the recent explosion of e-mails and instant and text messaging, and not many people pick up a pen nowadays. And even when we do, it's often to sign our name on a commercial greeting card. So for the most part, we're either communicating electronically or with someone else's words.

It's not too late to start writing again. If you wrote letters once, you'll find it's like riding a bicycle—you never forget how. For those of you who never wrote letters—now's a good time to start.

You say you're not a wordsmith? In this day of e-mails and store-bought greeting cards, not many people are. But a personal note can speak volumes. Nothing compares with a few lines written from the heart.

This book helps you write sincere, heartfelt notes for every occasion, from birthdays to bar mitzvahs. In the process, we hope you rediscover the lost art of letter writing.

How This Book Is Organized

This book is organized into 15 chapters that cover every type of short, personal letter you'll ever need to write. Each chapter contains dozens of sample notes you can use just as they are or adapt to fit your friends, family, or a particular situation. At the end of each chapter, we offer a list of inspirational and humorous quotes to spice up your correspondence.

Two appendixes at the end of the book discuss e-mail etiquette and list further resources you can peruse to help you write better notes.

Some Things to Help You Out Along the Way

Each chapter also includes sidebars with quick tips and handy hints to improve your letter-writing skills. Here's what to look for:

The Write Way

These suggestions help you hone your letter-writing skills and write memorable letters.

Greeting Goofs

These boxes tell you what *not* to write by pointing out common letter-writing blunders.

Acknowledgments

Veronica and Marylou would like to thank the following people: Alison Fargis of The Stonesong Press; Paul Dinas of Alpha Books; and our friends and families who, without realizing it, provided great material for this book. You're all in here. Thanks for the memories.

Trademarks

All terms mentioned in this book that are known to be or are suspected of being trademarks or service marks have been appropriately capitalized. Alpha Books and Penguin Group (USA) Inc. cannot attest to the accuracy of this information. Use of a term in this book should not be regarded as affecting the validity of any trademark or service mark.

Chapter 1

Birthdays

A birthday is a birthday, right? It doesn't matter whose it is. Wrong! It makes all the difference in the world. After all, you wouldn't send the same card to your elderly Aunt Adeline as you would to your friend Alexis who has a tattoo of a butterfly on her lower back and a ring in her navel. (Or would you?) More than 60 percent of the everyday cards sent each year in the United States are birthday cards, and senders add a personal message 70 percent of the time. If not knowing what to say is what's holding you back, the samples in this chapter can help you wish that someone special a happy birthday.

Let Age Be Your Gauge

Whether your birthday wishes are for a hip teen, a hippie 40-year-old, or a toddler with diapers on his hips, one of these notes—or your personalized version—should be a perfect fit.

To Toddlers

I heard a secret that you turned 2 today. Is it true? What a big boy you are! I hope your day is filled with thrills and fun surprises. Happy 2nd birthday!

The Write Way

Keep it short and sweet when writing to young children. They can't read by themselves, and words like *big boy* or rhyming words sound good when parents read them aloud.

Can you count to three? Because that's how old you are today! Let's try it. One ... two ... *three!* Three cheers for the birthday girl! Happy, happy, happy birthday!

You're 5! Hooray! You get 5 candles on your birthday cake! How great is that? Guess what? I think I'll send you 5 hugs and kisses, too. Have a happy birthday!

To Tweens

Wow! Nine years old today and getting more grown up every year. You're not just the star of the day, you're the coolest girl I know. I hope your birthday is a ton of fun and your wishes all come true. Happy birthday!

Ten is such a cool age to be. Just think—you're finally into the double digits! I hope your birthday goes just the way you want. Lots of presents, lots of friends, and lots of cake and ice cream! Happy 10th birthday!

Greeting Goofs

Don't talk down to children, no matter how young they are. Avoid sugary terms like *sweetie pie* or *dearest darling*. You'll only succeed in embarrassing them.

Hey there, tall, dark, and handsome. Oh well, two out of three ain't bad. Don't worry—in a few years, you'll be towering over me. Happy birthday, big boy!

To Teens

I hear you're 16 today. Does that mean you'll be on the road soon? Behind the wheel of a souped-up muscle car? Maybe drag racing? God help us all! Happy birthday, speed demon!

The Write Way

Writing a note to a teen is tricky. Keep it light and positive; maybe even go for a little humor. Getting too serious can be a turn-off. And whatever you do, cut the criticism.

I know 15-year-olds spend a lot of time online instant messaging their friends. Well, here's my instant message for you—happy birthday!

When you're 17, the world is an open book with all the pages waiting to be written. Your future is full of promise. Here's hoping that today's dreams will come true for you tomorrow. Have a sensational birthday.

To Twenty-Somethings

Because you're 22 today, you deserve an over-the-top weekend in Vegas with all your buds. Too bad we're all as broke as you are, so you'll have to settle for a six-pack and some poker at my place. Happy birthday anyway, dude.

It isn't easy being you. You're smart, chic, upwardly mobile, and you have a body that won't quit. It must be a distraction, turning heads everywhere you go. You won't be 25 forever, so live it up on your birthday!

Early American upstart Henry David Thoreau once said, "Go confidently in the direction of your dreams. Live the life you have imagined." That's my birthday wish for you today. Be an upstart like Thoreau. You'll never regret it.

The Write Way

A quote is a great way to start off a note. Just be sure it's appropriate. Check out the quotes at the end of this chapter for some inspiration, or turn to Appendix B at the end of the book for some more sources.

Birthday Milestones

On television, 16-year-olds get a car for their sweet 16. I got you a car, too! I just added a "d" to the end of it. Happy birthday!

You just turned 18, which means you're an adult now. Welcome to the grown-up club. I hope you still celebrate your day like a kid.

You're 21! You can order a drink (legally), gamble, and come home when you feel like it. Isn't it time to do your own laundry? Happy birthday from Mom (a.k.a. the laundress).

Georges Clemenceau once said, "Everything I know I learned after I was thirty." Have a fabulous birthday, and say hello to the best years ahead.

What's the best part of being 40? Greater wisdom and insight? Knowing what you want and how to get it? Having fun without being medicated? It's all reason to celebrate. So let those 40 candles glow, my friend. You have arrived! Happy birthday.

> **Greeting Goofs** _____
>
> People who turn 40 or 50 don't appreciate being told they're "over the hill." They may smile politely or pretend to laugh, but it's a safe bet they're not amused.

Stop the presses! The news is out! You're 50 today! I like to think of it as a warm-up for the next 50 years. So live, laugh, and love your birthday. You've earned every minute of it.

To Older People

French actress Brigitte Bardot was right when she said, "What could be more beautiful than a dear old lady growing wise with age?" Your face shines with a beauty that permeates everything you do and say. Have a wonderful time celebrating 82 years!

I heard you were turning 77 today. To me, you're like a fine wine—not getting older, just getting better. I hope your birthday is as special as you are.

Relationships Rule

Life is about connections—with parents, siblings, grandkids, friends, and spouses. These notes reveal how different each relationship can be.

To Sons/Daughters

I had such hopes for you when you were a child. Now that you're a woman, I'm thrilled to see they've all come true. You're kind, generous, hard-working, and dedicated, and you believe in yourself. You make me proud to call you my daughter. May your own hopes come true on your birthday and always.

The Write Way _____

Be sure your focus is on the other person. It's okay to throw in a few *I*'s or *we*'s, but *you* should be the word of choice.

When you were born, you were the light of my life. Now that you're an adult, it's time to step back and let you glow. Have a wonderful birthday.

To Parents

Dear Dad,

When it comes to fathers, you are the best of the best. No matter what happens, you're always there for me, a strong shoulder to lean on whenever I need it. So have a happy birthday, Dad—and can I borrow the car tonight?

Dear Dad,

I don't say this often enough, but thanks for all you've done for me. It's funny how you always seem to be there whenever I need you. I guess that's what being a father is all about. Have a great birthday, and promise me we'll celebrate for a long time to come. I still need you.

Dear Mom,

I learned so much from you as I was growing up. How to mow the lawn, repair a light switch, change the oil in the car, wash the dishes, ... oops that was Dad. Gotta give credit where it's due. Enjoy your birthday, Mom. Love ya.

Dear Mom,

You might think I'm not listening to you most of the time, but a lot more gets through than you realize. You see, you're my inspiration. I've watched how you live your own life, and I've held it up as an example for my own. So have a happy birthday, Mom. I hear ya.

To Stepparents

What's a stepmother to me? Someone who's smart, kind, funny, and patient. In a word, she's *you*. You're the best thing that could've happened to our family. Happy birthday.

There aren't too many people who could have come into our crazy family and fit in so comfortably. The fact that you succeeded is a tribute to your love and determination. Wishing you the finest of birthdays.

To Siblings

What can you say about a brother who is smart, good-looking, fun, patient, considerate, helpful, and an all-around nice guy? How about "Stay out of my room!" Just kidding. Happy birthday to the best brother in the world!

When I think of how much we shared when we were little—our bedroom, our clothes, our toys, our secrets—I wish we could go back to those carefree days. Now that we're on the subject, can I borrow your black dress tomorrow night? Happy birthday, sis!

To Grandparents

Dear Grandma,

Some of my fondest memories growing up were visits from you. You would tell me stories and we'd make cookies together. Let's get together soon and make a new batch. Happy birthday, Grandma.

The Write Way

Grandparents love it when you bring up the past. Personalizing these sample notes with your own experiences makes them even more special.

Dear Grandpa,

You made me the luckiest grandkid in the world. As I was growing up, you told me stories, taught me about life, and sneaked me money when no one was looking, and I will never forget it. Enjoy your birthday.

To Grandchildren

I know what you just did. Before you read this card, you shook it to see if money would fall out. And it did! I hope you enjoy the $25. I also hope you took a second to read this card so you'll know that my love for you is priceless.

I'll never forget the day I became your grandmother. You were so tiny, but I could see from the sparkle in your eye that you were a live wire. I admit there are times when being around you wears me out, but mostly you make me feel young again. Thank you for that lovely gift, birthday girl.

To Spouses

Little girls are supposed to be made of sugar and spice and everything nice, right? Well, someone must have tossed in a jalapeño pepper when you were growing up, hon. You are one hot tamale. Hope your birthday sizzles!

You know what I love about you most? Your laugh. No, I think it's your beautiful eyes. Wait, it's your inner strength. Hold it, it's the way you make friends with everyone you meet. No, it's your kissable lips. Know what? I love it all.

I knew I was lucky when I married you. You're so much more than I expected in a man. You're my adviser, husband, lover, and best friend. I hope your birthday brings you as much happiness as you've brought to me.

To Other Family

Dear Aunt,

What do I love about you? You always listen to me. Not just with your ears, but with your heart. You don't know how much it means to a kid who doesn't always know how to be heard. Have a lovely birthday, and thanks for letting me be myself.

Dear Uncle,

Somebody once said, "Families are like fudge—mostly sweet with a few nuts." There's no doubt you're the nut in our family, but we wouldn't have it any other way. Have a fun birthday!

Dear Niece,

I love having a niece like you. You're so full of life and fun that you make me smile all the time. Here's hoping your birthday is every bit as enjoyable as you are.

Dear Nephew,

He looks like an ordinary nephew on the outside, but inside he's really a superhero. Look, up in the sky! It's a bird! It's a plane! It's "Birthday Boy"!

To Friends

A toast to friendship. It's not important how many friends you have, but how much you value each one. Happy birthday to a friend I will always value. Cheers!

I once read that a good friend is someone who will always tell you the truth. Or was it a good friend is someone who will lie to make you feel good? Anyway, happy birthday to the smartest, best-looking, sexiest guy in the world.

The Write Way

Birthday humor is okay if it's aimed at a friend or close family member, especially if you're the same age. The older someone is, however, the less likely they are to be amused.

If I were really your friend: (a) I'd buy you an expensive present for your birthday, (b) I'd take you out to dinner, and (c) I'd let you know what a great guy you are. Unfortunately, I can't afford (a) or (b). Happy birthday anyway!

To Boyfriends/Girlfriends

Since I met you, my life has changed so much. You fill my heart with more love than I ever thought possible. I enjoy being close to you, sharing thoughts with you, and knowing that you are my best friend. Have a happy birthday, sweetheart.

Soulmate. I didn't believe it was possible—until I met you. You seem to know my thoughts and words before they come out of my mouth. I feel closer to you than to anyone I've ever known. I'm so happy to celebrate the day you came into this world so you could be with me.

To Co-Workers

Whether we're gossiping over coffee or telling bad jokes at the water cooler, I'd rather it was you than anyone else. I raise my cup of java in a toast to your birthday and many, many more.

It's such a pleasure to work with you. Your integrity and work ethic are beyond reproach. You've also been a mentor to everyone who works in our office. I offer my heartfelt congratulations on your 45th birthday.

Birthday Blessings

Sometimes a religious or spiritual note is just what you want to send. When you can't find your own words, try some of the following.

Religious

The Lord said, "Ask and it shall be given you; seek, and ye shall find." For your birthday this year, I pray that you will find God's peace, comfort, and joy in your life.

Greeting Goofs

Don't send a religious/spiritual card or note to someone who doesn't share your beliefs. When in doubt, stick to a simple birthday note that's sincere and personal.

I have the best news! God is sending his loving angels to watch over you on your birthday and every day this year. How do I know this? I asked him to!

Spiritual

I hope peace and harmony will be yours today—a day that celebrates your birth into the world. May the spirit of love reach out to you today and always.

Buddha once offered these wise words: "Do not dwell in the past, do not dream of the future, concentrate the mind on the present moment." Today is your birthday. Enjoy the moment.

I Forgot!

Forgetting a birthday is a no-no, so send a belated card or note as soon as you remember! Here are some samples you can use to send your birthday wishes— a little late.

I can't believe I missed your birthday! I was remembering and remembering ... and then I forgot! One thing I haven't forgotten is how special you are to me.

Greeting Goofs

Don't write a book about why you were late. Just let the person know you're sorry and end on a positive note.

Oh, no! I forgot your birthday. I guess I deserve a swift kick in the behind. I have only one request before you get started ... be gentle. Happy belated birthday!

Quotes to Inspire You

A diplomat is a man who always remembers a woman's birthday but never remembers her age. —*Robert Frost*

Birthdays are good for you. The more you have, the longer you live. —*Unknown*

Age is strictly a case of mind over matter. If you don't mind, it doesn't matter. —*Jack Benny*

You can only be young once. But you can always be immature. —*Dave Barry*

The advantage of being eighty years old is that one has many people to love. —*Jean Renoir*

We are always the same age inside. —*Gertrude Stein*

Old age is like everything else. To make a success of it, you've got to start young. —*Fred Astaire*

The more you praise and celebrate your life, the more there is in life to celebrate. —*Oprah Winfrey*

The lovely thing about being forty is that you can appreciate twenty-five-year-old men. —*Colleen McCullough*

Chapter 2

Anniversaries

You've probably heard the expression: marriage is like a merry-go-round; people are jumping on and off all the time. So why not give a cheer for the committed few who hang on to their horses despite the ups and downs? Here are some anniversary notes to make your family and friends—and your sweetheart—sit tall in the saddle on that special day.

Between You and Me

His *snoring keeps you awake at night and* her *shoe collection has taken over your closet. But after all these years, you still love each other. How do you put those feelings in a card?*

From Husbands to Wives

What can I say after 12 years of marriage, honey? You're the cream in my coffee, you're the butter on my toast, you're the apple of my eye, you're the cherry on my sundae … Gee, I'm hungry. What's for dinner tonight?

I'm so grateful to have you as my wife. You're a great friend, you make me feel important, and you're as beautiful as the day we met. I can't imagine life without you. Happy anniversary.

You're beautiful, talented, a great cook, a wonderful mother, and a fantastic lover. And best of all, you laugh at my jokes! Wait … that came out wrong. What I said before wasn't a joke. You really *are* all those things! Happy anniversary, Superwoman!

From Wives to Husbands

If I were stuck on a desert island and could only bring three prized possessions with me, what would they be? You, you, and you! Happy anniversary to the man who gives me everything I'll ever need.

How do I love you? Let me count the ways. I love (1) waking up beside you every morning, (2) holding your hand when I'm scared, (3) laying my tired head on your shoulder, (4) snuggling in bed with you at night, and (5) being your wife for 5 amazing years. Happy anniversary, Sweetheart!

The Write Way

Make a list of all the little things your husband or wife does for you. A few words of appreciation can produce a smile—or a tear—every time.

Last night I dreamed you were a knight in shining armor riding a white horse. You swept me into the saddle, and I could feel the wind billowing under my gown …. And then I woke up freezing because you were hogging all the covers! Happy anniversary to the man of my dreams.

To Both of Us

Phil Collins must've been talking about us when he wrote the song lyrics "Two hearts, believing in just one mind / Beating together till the end of time." I love that we're still so close. Happy anniversary to us—a great duet.

People say we're made for each other. Let's hope that's a compliment! But as long as we keep living in a fool's paradise, who cares? Happy anniversary to a couple "fools" for love.

The Ties That Bind

You may not get to choose your families. But if you didn't have their anniversaries to celebrate, you wouldn't be here in the first place! And what about your friends? You know you really love 'em all, so why not let them know?

To Parents

You balance each other so well. Your humor, your personalities, your approaches to life. It's like you're yin and yang. I can't imagine one of you without the other. Hope your anniversary is as fabulous as you two are.

It's time for the truth. You're too affectionate for this stage of your marriage. You grab each other when you think no one's looking. You kiss and hug all the time. C'mon, guys! Act your age. Aww ... what the heck. It's your anniversary. Go for it, lovebirds!

Happy anniversary to the couple who brought me into the world, nurtured me, encouraged me, and then kicked me out of the nest when it was time. You made me the strong, independent person I am today.

P.S. Can I move back home for a few months? (Just kidding!)

The Write Way

Anniversary notes can be humorous. You can even gently poke fun at the foibles of people close to you. But always include how much the couple means to you and say something positive about their marriage.

To Grandparents

Life is such an adventure for you two and your curiosity knows no bounds. You try new things. You travel to new places. You're always on the go. Hope your anniversary is as thrilling as you are.

Every family needs a solid foundation, and none is more solid than the one you've built. Yours is a marriage of love, trust, tolerance, and commitment. Thanks for showing us the right way to do it. Happy anniversary.

The poet Robert Browning wrote, "Grow old along with me, the best is yet to be." You two live your best lives and make the most of every day, and you always have. Here's to your wonderful marriage—past, present, and future.

To Parents and Stepparents

Dear Dad and _____,

The day you married, our two families became one. You've taught us that living and working together is more fun than going it alone. On your anniversary, I want to wish you many more years of fun and togetherness.

Greeting Goofs _____

Don't include any information about yourself in the note. Keep your focus on the couple, their relationship, and the occasion. Remember, it's their day you're celebrating, not yours.

Dear Mom and _____,

Best wishes on your 4th wedding anniversary. It seems like only yesterday the two of you met, because you still act like a couple of newlyweds. My mom was lucky to find a man who makes her so happy. Have a beautiful day.

To Sons/Daughters and Their Spouses

To me, your marriage is like an oak tree—rooted in love and growing more solid every year. So maybe you'll start adding some little branches soon?

You two lovebirds seemed so young and innocent when you walked down the aisle. But with 5 years of wedded bliss under your belts, you'll be joining the army of old married folks soon. Welcome to the ranks, from the General and her husband.

To Siblings and Their Spouses

Here's an anniversary toast to my dear sister and brother-in-law. May your days be filled with sunshine, laughter, and continued wedded bliss. You'll need it with all the kids you're planning to have! Enjoy your anniversary while you still can!

Greeting Goofs _____

Avoid stereotypical jokes or humorous remarks about the problems of marriage. You want to praise the couple, not insult them.

You wanna know the secret of true love? What are you asking me for? You could write a book on the subject! Happy anniversary to the most loving married couple I know.

To Friends

To celebrate the anniversary of a couple of friends, you need to be really close. So close that you know everything about their marriage. Don't worry. Your secret is safe with us. Got you wondering now, haven't we?

You can count on best friends to tell you the truth about yourselves. Well, here goes: you two were made for each other. Anniversary wishes to the happiest couple we know—other than us!

Anniversary Milestones

Maybe nobody told you guys yet, but the honeymoon is over! So cut the lovey-dovey stuff. You're gonna ruin it for the rest of us old married folks. Happy 1st anniversary to a couple who can't keep their hands off each other.

When you did that high dive into the marriage pool years ago, did you think you'd score a perfect 10? Congratulations on 10 years of togetherness. Here's looking to 20!

The Write Way

Looking for an upbeat way to end your note? Try offering good wishes for the future. It reminds people that marriage is an ongoing commitment and gives them hope for what's to come.

You're our dearest friends, and it's a thrill to send you our congratulations for 25 years of marriage. May your anniversary be as unforgettable as the day you took your vows. Happy silver anniversary!

What an amazing accomplishment! You've been married for 50 years today. Every moment of your life together has shown such grace and dignity that you inspire us all. Your anniversary is truly golden.

After 60 years of marriage, my memories are as precious as the diamond you first gave me. They make me fall in love with you all over again. Happy anniversary, my darling.

Promises, Promises

Not everyone commits to marriage. Some people date for a while and others live in long-term committed relationships—out of choice or necessity. A commitment is a commitment, no matter how you look at it. If the impulse strikes, here are some words to write.

For Dating Relationships

I can't believe we've been dating 2 years. I feel as if I've known you forever! Thanks for all the happiness and fun you've brought into my life. Happy "2nd" anniversary.

When I met you 6 months ago, I thought, *Wow, what a knockout!* I still feel that way. You knock me out, baby, and I'm lovin' it! Happy 6-month anniversary.

For Committed Relationships

After 20 years together, you two are more committed than any couple I know. You've become life partners in the true sense of the word. Happy anniversary. Looking forward to the next 20!

As Steve Martin would put it, "You're a couple of wild and crazy guys!" Your relationship gets more entertaining as the years go by. When you two are around, the laughter's contagious. I'd tell you to have a fun anniversary, but I'm sure it's already in the works!

Greeting Goofs

Avoid comments like "you might as well be married" to committed couples who aren't. Respect for other people's lifestyle is a must.

Good for You!

Committing yourself to the same job for 25 years is quite an accomplishment. So are other life-changing accomplishments like quitting smoking. We think a few words of congratulations are in order!

For Job-Related Accomplishments

Congratulations on 25 years with the company. You've been more than an asset, and you've earned the respect and affection of your colleagues. We couldn't have accomplished half of what we did without you. Looking forward to many more years of success.

Is it true? You're celebrating 20 years in the office? You've been my right hand for so long I sometimes feel you're an extension of me. I mean that as a compliment. Your good sense and wisdom have come through for me more than once. I know I'd be lost without you. Here's hoping you'll stay for another 20!

For Life-Changing Accomplishments

You did it! And not just for 1 year, but for an unbelievable 5 years! It took a lot of strength and willpower for you to take off those extra pounds and keep them off. You're a role model for all of us. Happy 5th anniversary!

> ### The Write Way
> People can be sensitive (and rightfully so) about past problems. Write a note only if you know your recipient well and he or she has discussed the problem with you.

I can't believe it's been 5 years since you quit smoking. When I gave you the gift certificate for hypnosis, I wasn't sure how you'd react. But you gave it a try, and you haven't taken a puff since! Congratulations on kicking the habit. I'm proud of you.

Just wanted to congratulate you for being dry for 2 years. Your stick-to-itiveness has been impressive. It's nice to have our old friend back again. We missed him. Happy 2nd anniversary!

Anniversary Blessings

Spiritual cards are lovely and sometimes the most appropriate words you can send. Be sure your recipient will appreciate them, though.

Religious

"It is not good that man should be alone, I will make him a helper as his partner." (Genesis 2:18) You live together, love together, work together, and play together. Your marriage is a partnership in every sense of the word. God bless you on your anniversary.

"Arise, come, my darling; my beautiful one, come with me." (Song of Solomon 2:13) These words describe how I feel about you every morning of our life together. I'm so happy we made this journey together. Happy anniversary to my darling, my beautiful one, my love.

> **The Write Way** _____
>
> Bible verses and other quotes are an effective way of starting a religious or spiritual card. There are a lot of them out there, including the ones at the end of this chapter. Find one that inspires you, and take it from there.

Spiritual

If a good marriage must be created, you two are masters of the art. You've shaped a union of such beauty and simplicity that people around you can't help but smile at your accomplishment.

"Let us be grateful to people who make us happy, they are the charming gardeners who make our souls blossom." (Marcel Proust) You make me happier than I ever thought possible. And my soul? It wants to burst into flower every time I'm with you. Happy anniversary to the gardener of my dreams.

I Forgot!

You did it. You forgot an anniversary. But don't feel bad, it does happen. Just apologize and move on to the compliments—fast.

Oops. Looks like I missed our anniversary. I'd call it a "senior moment" but I'm only 27! I feel really bad because I love you so much and I'm grateful to get to spend every day with you. Happy late anniversary to the only girl for me.

How could I forget your anniversary? I even tied a string around my finger … but then I forgot why I tied it. Well, I don't need a string to remind me what a fabulous couple you are. Hope your anniversary was the best. And don't worry—next year I'm tying two strings!

Quotes to Inspire You

Marriage is not just spiritual communion, it is also remembering to take out the trash. —*Joyce Brothers*

There is no greater happiness for a man than approaching a door at the end of a day knowing someone on the other side of that door is waiting for the sound of his footsteps. —*Ronald Reagan*

Married couples who love each other tell each other a thousand things without talking. —*Chinese proverb*

My most brilliant achievement was my ability to be able to persuade my wife to marry me. —*Winston Churchill*

Our wedding was many years ago. The celebration continues to this day. —*Humorist Gene Perret*

Chains do not hold a marriage together. It is threads, hundreds of tiny threads, which sew people together through the years. —*Simone Signoret*

A good marriage is a contest of generosity. —*Diane Sawyer*

Love seems the swiftest, but it is the slowest of all growths. No man or woman really knows what perfect love is until they have been married a quarter of a century. —*Mark Twain*

Chapter 3

Weddings and Engagements

When a man pops the big question and a woman says yes, it sets off a chain reaction of announcements, requests, RSVPs, congratulation cards, and thank you notes. The printed material generated by each marriage proposal would probably reach around the world—twice. And when you consider that about 2.4 million weddings are performed each year in the United States, the number of notes being written can boggle the mind! If writing that one special note is boggling *your* mind, this chapter should provide plenty of inspiration.

He Proposed! She Said Yes!

The children's verse goes, "First comes love, then comes marriage ..." But in between comes the engagement. Whether you're announcing your engagement or responding to the good news, the following notes help you find the perfect words to express your happiness.

Spreading the News

Justin finally proposed! And I said yes, yes, yes! We're having an engagement party/barbecue at my parents' house on May 21 at 5 P.M. Can you come and celebrate with us? Hope your answer is yes, yes, yes!

> **Greeting Goofs**
>
> Don't send engraved engagement announcements listing the date of your wedding—people might think they're wedding invitations. Stick to handwritten announcements or buy cards that say "We're Engaged!" and add a personal note.

Please join us on September 25 to celebrate the engagement of our son, Dan, to Jessica King, the wonderful girl he fell in love with. Cocktails and hors d'oeuvres will be served at 4 P.M. at the home of Paul and Ellen Hamilton. Please RSVP by September 20.

To the Bride-to-Be

Engaged! I'm so excited for you, words escape me. Except for this one: *congratulations!* Oh, and these three: *when's the wedding?* And these five: *you'll make a beautiful bride.* Best wishes from your speechless friend.

He popped the question—what wonderful news! We couldn't be happier if you were our own daughter. This is one engagement party we won't miss. We've been hearing for months about your special young man, and now we can't wait to meet him.

The Write Way _____

When responding to an engagement announcement, always be considerate. Write a note you'd want to receive yourself, maybe even keep in your scrapbook forever.

To the Groom-to-Be

Wow! So you finally found Miss Right. What a relief! We had visions of you old and alone, with no one for company but your cat. Seriously, Nancy and I are very happy for you and we can't wait to meet Melissa. We promise not to embarrass you by telling high school stories or showing her any dorky pictures of you. Well, maybe just a few ...

When your mother told me you were engaged, I just about burst my buttons, I was so proud. Does your fiancée have any idea what a wonderful young man she's getting? She must or she wouldn't have said "yes." Your uncle and I can't wait to kick up our heels and celebrate with you.

Greeting Goofs _____

Uh oh. Your aunt is marrying a guy half her age. Don't comment on this in your note! Find something upbeat to say even if you have doubts about the marriage.

To the Parents of the Couple

We're thrilled to hear about Danielle's engagement. You've had your fingers crossed for a while, so you must be giddy with joy. We still have the planning book from Pam's wedding last year and would be delighted to loan it to you until you start your own. Thanks for sharing the good news!

I hear you're going to be the mother of a groom! How exciting! If the kids are planning a formal wedding, I know just where you can get the perfect gown—at a huge discount. I can't wait to go shopping with you!

From the Parents to the Couple

Since you and Jennifer told us about your engagement, we've been walking on air! We're overjoyed that you found such a lovely and talented young woman to be your bride. We welcome her into our family with open arms.

So your Prince Charming proposed. That doesn't surprise us one bit. How could he not fall madly in love with our beautiful and brilliant princess? We hope you two have a storybook wedding and live happily ever after.

From the Grandparents to the Couple

George Bernard Shaw said, "Youth is wasted on the young." We disagree. We savored every intoxicating moment of our courtship, engagement, and wedding; then we felt the same excitement when our children got married. Now it's happening again! Take it from the voice of experience—youth is a wonderful time to be in love. Don't waste a minute of it.

When you were born, our hearts were filled with love and pride. That hasn't changed. One of the proudest moments of our lives will be seeing you walk down the aisle.

From In-Laws to In-Laws

How wonderful that our children found each other and fell in love! They say you don't marry a person, you marry a family, and we can't think of a nicer, more loving family for our Rachael to marry than yours.

We were thrilled when the kids told us they were engaged. Your daughter Diane is such a delight, it's no wonder our son fell in love with her. We can't wait to meet you, too. Why don't we all have dinner at our house next weekend to celebrate?

Wedding Bliss

As the wedding day approaches, more writing opportunities present themselves (we like to think of them as opportunities, not chores). The possibilities seem endless—but your search for the right words doesn't have to be. Keep reading for ideas.

To the Wedding Couple

It's your wedding day: an end and a beginning. The end of all the planning you've done for the past few months … and the beginning of all the new planning you'll do as a married couple! Enjoy your special day and the lifetime you'll have together.

 Greeting Goofs _____

> Weddings bring out the incurable romantic in us, but don't get carried away with stilted or flowery language, or you'll sound insincere.

Weddings are like champagne. You start by feeling all bubbly inside, and you end up drunk with happiness. Here's a magnum of sparkling joy to celebrate your special day.

The countdown is over! It's time to get married! You probably won't read this until after the honeymoon, so I hope your day was dynamite and your honeymoon was a blast. Let me know when you get the wedding video. I'll supply the popcorn!

To the Parents of the Couple

Congratulations on the wedding of your daughter. It must give you great joy to know that she's marrying such a terrific guy. I hope their life together will be blessed with much love and happiness.

> **The Write Way**
>
> Weddings are a family affair. A few words of congratulations to the parents or grandparents of the bride and groom are usually appreciated.

You're the father of the bride. Remember, you're not losing a daughter; you're gaining a son to lift all the heavy stuff you can't handle anymore. Congratulations, you lucky guy!

To the Grandparents of the Couple

Congratulations on your grandson's wedding. Thanks to our friendship, we watched him grow from a spunky little boy into a handsome and talented man. You must be very proud of him. Thank you for inviting us to join in the celebration.

Another year, another wedding. How many of those grandkids have you married off already? Five? Six? You must be pleased as punch to get another corsage to wear. Well, if I had grandparents like you, I'd want to show you off, too. Congrats on the latest nuptials!

From the Bride to the Groom

You are the best thing that ever happened to me. You're my best friend, my lover, and my soul mate. Words can't express how much I love you today. You are my hero, and I can't wait to see your handsome face when I walk down the aisle to become your wife.

It's finally here, honey, the day we've been waiting for. If I get cold feet I promise I'll still marry you, because I need you to warm them up at night. The truth is, my feet warm up just thinking of you. All of me does, 'cause I'm crazy about you—today and always.

From the Groom to the Bride

I'm not great with words, honey, so I'm going to keep this simple. I love you a bunch, I need you a bunch, and I want you a bunch. How soon can we start the honeymoon?

I never imagined I'd meet anyone who understood me the way you do. You always know the right thing to say, whether I'm feeling good or bad. And you're going to marry me! I'm the luckiest guy in the world. See you at the church.

From the Bride to the Bridesmaids

It would mean so much to me if you'd walk down the aisle at my wedding wearing a bridesmaid's gown. I promise not to pick something hideous! Whether you can be my bridesmaid or not, I know I can count on your love and support that day.

I can't imagine getting married without you standing next to me as my maid of honor. I hope you'll say yes. We've shared so much together throughout our friendship, it only seems right that you're with me as I say "I do" to my husband.

From the Groom to the Groomsmen

You stood by me through good times and bad. How about standing by me as best man on the best, most important day of my life? The tux is on me—that is, I'll foot the bill!

Want a ticket to the hottest wedding in town? All you have to do is be one of my groomsmen. The bridesmaids are all smokin' so there's a 100 percent chance of escorting a gorgeous female down the aisle. How can you refuse an offer like that?

From the Parents to the Bride

It seems like only yesterday you were a little girl playing bride with a handful of daisies. Now you're all grown up and walking down the aisle for real. You were beautiful then, and you're even more beautiful now. Congratulations, big girl.

If you see me crying when you walk down the aisle today, know that they're tears of joy, not sorrow. I'm watching my smart, beautiful daughter marry the man she loves. What more could a mother ask for? Have a wonderful life together.

From the Parents to the Groom

Now that your wedding day is here, I have some fatherly advice to share with you: respect your wife, be patient and thoughtful, buy her little gifts often, and tell her you love her every day. But most of all—and never, never, never, forget this—she's *always* right!

Today you're setting off on the great adventure called marriage. You'll have ups and downs, just like your father and I did, but you'll find that the good times make up for the bad. Sharing life's journey with someone you love always makes it sweeter. Have a truly memorable wedding, son.

From Parents to the Couple

In 1970, a book/movie called *Love Story* by Eric Segal immortalized the line, "Love means never having to say you're sorry." Hogwash. Love means admitting when you're wrong and being man or woman enough to say "I'm sorry." Welcome to the greatest love story of your life.

The Write Way

Greeting cards use them all the time—why shouldn't you use them in your notes? We're talking about quotes. Go to Google and type in "love quotes." We found 64,500,000 sites! That should be enough to get you started.

Today's the day! You approached your wedding with such a sense of teamwork, you must be meant for each other. You'll be finishing each other's sentences by your first anniversary! If this is a hint of what your future life will be like, your marriage will be a great success!

From the Couple to Their Parents

There are no words to express our deep appreciation for the beautiful wedding you gave us. It was the best day of our lives, and we'll never forget it—or forget what you two did to make it come true. We love you both very much.

Thanks a million for helping us throw the "wedding of the year"! We couldn't have pulled it off without your help and support. We'll be basking in the glow of that perfect day for months and years to come. We love you!

Responses to Invitations

Come to your wedding? A stampede of wild elephants wouldn't keep me away! If it's anything like the last time we partied, we'll probably close down the place—permanently. Count me in, pal.

The Write Way

Most people just check off the "I accept" or "I regret" box on a wedding invitation reply card. But if you were the bride, wouldn't you be pleasantly surprised to find a brief handwritten note as well?

We'd love to accept your wedding invitation. We hear the groom is quite a catch, but we think the bride is, too. We look forward to meeting your young man and seeing both of you walk down the aisle as man and wife.

Oh no! We're attending our granddaughter's baptism out of state the weekend of your wedding. We're so disappointed we can't be there for your big day, but we'll be thinking of you and celebrating from afar.

Commitment Ceremonies

Not every couple fits the traditional picture of the young, blushing bride and groom. Older couples are renewing their vows, same-sex couples are exchanging vows, and some couples feel they can make a commitment without marrying. The following sections give you ideas for responding to such commitment ceremonies.

Response to Invitation

A commitment ceremony! How wonderful. We think you and Howard wrote the book on commitment. We couldn't be happier for you. Thank you for including us in your special day.

Attend your commitment ceremony? We can't wait. You two have been inseparable for years now. It's about time you made it official. We wouldn't miss it for the world.

To the Couple

Promises! Promises! Sounds like a great title for a musical. It's also a great way to show the world how much you mean to each other. Can't thank you enough for letting me be a part of the celebration.

> ### Greeting Goofs
>
> Notes to nontraditional couples needn't be nontraditional themselves. Couples exchanging vows in commitment ceremonies appreciate the same heartfelt words as anyone else.

How lovely that the two of you have found each other at this time in your lives. You've both known the sadness of loss and yet know how sweet it is to love again. Congratulations on the commitment you are making to each other today.

Wedding Blessings

Marriage is one of life's "blessed events." So if the spirit moves you, send a religious or spiritual note.

Religious

In 1 Corinthians 13:7, Paul says, "Love never gives up, never loses faith, is always hopeful, and endures through every circumstance." I pray that the words of love you exchange with each other today will sustain you forever.

A marriage made in heaven is one that embraces God as a member. Think of yourselves not as a couple, but a threesome, with God's love joining you together. I pray that our Lord will be part of your marriage always.

Spiritual

The poet Kahlil Gibran once wrote, "Let there be spaces in your togetherness / And let the winds of heaven dance between you." Remember those words as you join together on your wedding day. It is only when you allow people the freedom to be themselves that they are willing to be one with you.

There's nothing more natural than love. You cannot force it. You must allow it to come of its own accord. Keep your hearts and minds open, and love will always find you.

Quotes to Inspire You

Now join hands, and with your hands, your hearts. —*William Shakespeare*

Rituals are important. Nowadays it's not hip to be married. I'm not interested in being hip. —*John Lennon*

Love is composed of a single soul inhabiting two bodies. —*Aristotle*

[W]hen you realize you want to spend the rest of your life with somebody, you want the rest of your life to start as soon as possible. —*Nora Ephron in* When Harry Met Sally

Love does not consist of gazing at each other, but in looking together in the same direction. —*Antoine de Saint-Exupéry*

If you live to be a hundred, I want to live to be a hundred minus one day, so I never have to live without you. —*A. A. Milne from* Winnie the Pooh

A successful marriage requires falling in love many times, always with the same person. —*Germaine Greer*

Chapter 4

It's All New to Me

The word *beginnings* evokes images of sunrises, spring flowers, and the first day of school. It can mean everything from having (or adopting) a baby, to starting a new job, to buying a new home. When friends and family embark on a new life adventure, help them celebrate by sending a note that says, "I'm excited for you!" The notes in this chapter give you some fresh ways to express your feelings.

A New Baby

Nothing's newer than a newborn baby or newsier than the announcement that someone's "expecting." But don't wait for the delivery date to deliver your congratulations. Use the following notes for ideas on how to announce—and reply to—news that a baby is on the way.

We're Having a Baby!

At last! An heir to the Webster family fortune! We're thrilled to announce that on December 20, we're expecting a bouncing baby boy! We're still weak at the knees but gathering our strength for the challenge of parenthood. We welcome any and all advice or words of wisdom!

Sit down. Are you ready? We're pregnant again! That's right. Expecting. With child. Bun in the oven. We couldn't be happier, and neither could Travis, who's already picking out names for his new brother or sister. Oh! The due date is October 19. We'll keep you posted ….

To the Parents-to-Be

A baby's on the way! Is there any more joyous news than this? Pregnancy is such an exciting time, but it can't compare to the wonder of finally holding that baby in your arms. Get ready for the best time of your lives!

The Write Way

When writing a note to an expectant couple, always be encouraging. Keep it to yourself if you think it's too soon to have a baby, or too late, or a crazy idea because they already have three kids.

I heard another little bundle of joy was arriving at your house on October 19. Fantastic! You and Ed must be thrilled, and I'll bet Jacob is telling all his school friends. Watch out—next he'll be taking your ultrasound photos to show and tell!

We Had a Delivery!

The National Center for Health Statistics reported 4,115,590 babies were born in the United States in 2004. That means millions of people sat with pens poised over cards, searching for the right words. You won't be one of them if you check out these notes.

To Babies

To my long-awaited grandson, with a million hugs and kisses—and a million thanks to my wonderful daughter and son-in-law for making it possible!

The Write Way

> Here's a tip for parents: save your babies' letters in a baby book. As adults, they can enjoy reading those special "first letters" from the special people in their life.

You're probably wondering, *Who are all these strangers making silly faces and noises at me?* We're your family, and we've waited a long time to meet you. Now that you're here, we're a little crazy—about you! Welcome to the world, baby girl!

To the Parents

I can't be there to hold Lily in my arms, so I did the next best thing. I knit her a fluffy pink sweater to wear close to her heart. When she has it on, I hope she'll know, somehow, that it's like my arms are around her.

The poet and novelist George Santayana said, "The family is one of nature's masterpieces." Congratulations on your latest masterpiece.

> **Greeting Goofs**
>
> Don't send a generic note or card that just says "Congratulations." Always include something personal about the family and the baby, such as the baby's name or the siblings' names.

To the Grandparents

What's this I hear about you being grandparents again? You obviously did something right when you were raising your kids, because they couldn't wait to have families of their own! Here's to you—great parents and great grandparents. (Not to be confused with great-grandparents—but that'll come in time!)

You're finally a grandparent! I hear it's even better than being a parent. You get to play with your grandkids as long as you want, spoil them as much as you want, and go home whenever you want! Congratulations. You've arrived.

To Siblings

You got a new baby sister? How cool is that? Sure, things are kind of hectic around your house, but I'll bet you aren't bored! How lucky your mom and dad are to have two big kids like you to help out. Congratulations on your new sister and new lifelong friend!

> **The Write Way**
>
> Siblings can feel neglected when a new baby arrives. Find a way to mention them by name in your note, such as, "I'll bet Megan is drawing pictures of her new baby brother and putting them on the fridge." Or write a note to the siblings. They'll love it!

I heard you just became a big brother. All right! Think of all the things you can teach your new little brother—how to catch frogs, how to squirt soda out your nose, how to hide your peas under your plate …. Lots of love and happy wishes to the *only* child who just became the *older* child.

For the First Child

Your first child! I don't think anyone is fully prepared for the shock and wonder of becoming a parent for the first time. Between the sleepless nights and the overwhelming love and responsibility, you're on an emotional roller coaster. Enjoy the ride, because she'll grow up fast!

There's nothing like that first baby. It's like enjoying a swim in warm ocean waters. Don't worry about getting in over your head. You'll be riding the waves in no time. Best wishes for your new baby.

For Boys

The old rhyme says little boys are made of "frogs and snails and puppy dog tails." What—like that's a bad thing? Mothers of sons wouldn't trade the frogs for all the Barbie dolls in the world. Here's to boys!

Oh, boy! It's a boy. Are you going to be a modern mom who teaches her son how to cook and clean and wash the dishes? Good for you! He'll make some lucky girl a perfect husband!

For Girls

The old rhyme says little girls are made of "sugar and spice and everything nice." Oh yeah? Mothers of daughters will tell you girls are a lot more spicy than sugary—and they wouldn't have it any other way. Here's to girls!

It's a girl! How lovely. She's a baby now, but one day she'll be listening to your heart with her toy stethoscope and repairing your dishwasher with a plastic screwdriver from her tool kit. It's a new world out there! Enjoy!

For Twins

In 2003, 128,665 twin births occurred in the United States. The numbers aren't out yet for this year, but no matter how many there were, Maria Elizabeth and Michael Edward Smith are two in a million!

The Write Way

Looking for an interesting fact or statistic about babies to insert in your note? Search the Net. Google "multiple births," and you'll come up with almost 2,000,000 sites.

Twins? Is it true? That means double the loving and double the fun! Then again, it means double the diapers and double the 4 A.M. feedings! But who's counting? Just get a diaper service and remember you're twice blessed. Congrats! Congrats!

We're Adopting!

Adoptions have been taking place since biblical times. Look at Moses, for example. If Pharaoh's daughter hadn't taken him in, he wouldn't have lived to lead his people to the Promised Land. Here are a few ways you can write to a family who've adopted a child, from either this country or abroad.

To Adopted Babies

You traveled halfway across the globe to a world of happiness that was waiting to greet you. Your mother and father love you, and your grandparents (that's us) can't wait to spoil you. Isn't the world a wonderful place?

The first time we saw your picture, we fell madly in love with you. We just knew you had to be our son. A few months later, a miracle happened. You arrived and now you *are* our son. I just love happy endings!

To the Parents

Someone once said, "Adoption is when a child grew in his mommy's heart instead of her tummy." May your precious child fill your hearts with joy every day of your lives.

 Greeting Goofs _____

Don't ask questions about the adopted child's biological or racial background—or her previous living conditions. She's part of the family now, and that's all that counts.

Were those hearts I saw floating over your house today? Rumor has it your new baby arrived and you're officially a mommy and a daddy. The gift of life is always worth the wait. Treasure this moment always.

To Adopted Older Children

We're so proud to have you in our family. A lifetime with you is what we've been hoping for, and it's finally come true. You are our son—the four most magical words in the world. Welcome!

The Write Way _____

A short welcome note to an older adopted child will make him feel even more special. Choose your card with care. Avoid the "a" word and let him know how happy you are that he's arrived.

To have a daughter like you is a dream come true. When you have your own children someday, you'll know how important this is to us. With you, our family is complete.

Baby Footnotes

Not every woman conceives naturally; 45,000 in vitro babies are born each year in the United States. And did you know that 8 to 10 percent of all pregnancies result in a premature baby? What about the babies born with major health issues—from diabetes to Down syndrome and birth defects? Here are some notes appropriate for such situations.

For In Vitro Babies

I don't know anyone who wanted a baby more than you two. In spite of all the obstacles, you never gave up. Thanks to modern science—and your determination—you now have a beautiful baby girl. May the three of you find all the happiness you deserve.

Hallelujah! It's a boy. It's been a tough haul, but you did it! Someday your new son will learn how hard his mother and father worked to give him life. Won't you be proud to tell him! Best wishes on your new family.

For Premature Babies

So your new baby boy surprised you by coming a month early? Just couldn't wait to meet his amazing parents, I guess. We hope he'll be home with you soon. If you need any help getting the nursery ready, give us a call. Hauling baby furniture is our specialty.

Congratulations on your new baby girl! Rachel has a big cheering section, hoping she gets out of intensive care soon. If there's anything we can do—like babysitting so you can go to the hospital—just let us know. Our good wishes are with you.

For Babies with Health Problems and Special Needs

We just learned about the birth of your daughter, Gina. We understand there may be some health concerns and wanted you to know that you and Gina are in our thoughts and prayers.

Greeting Goofs

The worst thing you can do is *not* write when a friend has a baby with a problem. At times like these, they need all the support you can give. Don't fixate on the problem or promise the child will be fine. Just be positive and offer help if you can.

When we heard about Adam's birth we were thrilled. Your mother tells us that he may have some medical problems. It's good to have friends around when challenges come up, so if we can help in any way—rides to the doctor or hospital, dinner, babysitting—please let us know. We love you and want to be there for you.

Baby Blessings

There's no greater blessing than the birth of a baby. If you're a religious or spiritual person and your recipient is, too, feel free to send a card expressing these sentiments.

Religious

Poet Carl Sandberg said, "A baby is God's opinion that the world should go on." How true! May God bless your family and the new life you've brought into the world.

Charles Dickens once said, "I love these little people, and it is not a slight thing when they who are so fresh from God love us." Next time I talk to God, I'll tell him, "Thanks a million for sending such a beautiful angel to Earth."

Spiritual

Each minute, all over the world, a baby is born. Each baby is one of life's miracles. And each little miracle brings a message from the universe—perfect love is possible. Congratulations on having your own little miracle.

The poet Kahlil Gibran wrote, "Your children are not your children. They are the sons and daughters of Life's longing for itself." How fortunate that our longing results in the joys of parenthood. May your new daughter experience her own longings and joys one day.

Off to a Fresh Start

The people in your life start new jobs, move to new homes, go to new schools, buy new cars, and adopt new pets. Celebrate these fresh starts by sending notes like the ones shown here.

For a New Job

Check out this Fats Domino quote: "A lot of fellows nowadays have a B.A., M.D., or Ph.D. Unfortunately, they don't have a J.O.B." Yeah, but *you* have a J.O.B. Congratulations! I gotta hand it to you. You put yourself out there and it paid off. How about buying me a drink to celebrate—you can afford it now!

I just heard the good news. Congratulations! It was always your dream to work in the fashion industry, and now you're doing it! You'll go far, once your boss sees how smart and talented you are. Don't forget us little people when you get there. It's my dream to buy designer clothes someday—at cost!

For a New Home

You bought a house! Congrats! How does it feel to be king of a three-bedroom castle instead of lowly serf in a studio rental? Did you replace the torn director's chair with a throne yet? Can't wait to see the new place. Hey … I'm free tomorrow. I'll bring dinner. It's my housewarming gift to you.

\   **The Write Way** _____

Getting a new home or job is no small potatoes; it requires a huge investment of time and money. Let your friends and family know how proud you are of their accomplishment.

That famous poet "Unknown" wrote: "It takes hands to build a house, but only hearts can build a home." Hooray! You finally moved into your new house. What started out as a "handyman special" turned into a showplace. Guess this is a case where both hands *and* hearts were involved!

For a New School

I heard Alex was accepted to law school. What a thrill for you to have a son who's going to be a lawyer. You must be so proud. Law school is tough, but with Alex's gift for debate, his professors better watch out. Tell him congratulations for me.

Wow! I just heard you were accepted into the resort management program at Green Mountain College in Vermont. Talk about a ski bum's dream come true! Between polishing your skis and checking out the snow bunnies, try to crack the books once in a while, okay? Here's to you, you lucky dog.

For a New Pet

A new puppy! Your kids (and you) must be thrilled. Welcome to the world of house training and obedience classes. Just stick to your guns, and he'll behave in no time. Meanwhile, think of the perks! You'll get plenty of fun—and exercise! Can't wait to see the little bundle of fur. Send me a picture soon.

You adopted a cat! Congrats! There's nothing more peaceful than a cat sleeping in your lap. And it's so easy to make them happy. A paper bag will keep her busy (and you in stitches) for hours. Have a *purr*fect time with your new friend.

Quotes to Inspire You

Quotes about babies and children:

Babies aren't born of their parents, they're born of every kind word, loving gesture, hope and dream their parents ever had. Bliss. —*Julia Roberts*

Children are our most valuable natural resource. —*Herbert Hoover*

The God to whom little boys say their prayers has a face very like their mother's. —*J. M. Barrie*

Thank heaven for little girls / they grow up in the most delightful way! —*Alan J. Lerner and Frederick Loewe in* Gigi

Children make you want to start life over. —*Muhammad Ali*

It takes a village to raise a child. —*African proverb*

Making the decision to have a child is momentous. It is to decide forever to have your heart go walking around outside your body. —*Elizabeth Stone*

Nobody can do for little children what grandparents do. Grandparents sort of sprinkle stardust over the lives of little children. —*Alex Haley*

Quotes about fresh starts:

The secret to a rich life is to have more beginnings than endings. —*Dave Weinbaum*

Choose a job you love and you will never have to work a day in your life. —*Confucius*

Home is the place where, when you have to go there, they have to take you in. —*Robert Frost*, The Death of the Hired Hand

Education is what remains after one has forgotten what one learned in school. —*Albert Einstein*

Education's purpose is to replace an empty mind with an open one. —*Malcolm S. Forbes*

Never drive faster than your guardian angel can fly. —*Unknown*

Animals are such agreeable friends—they ask no questions, they pass no criticisms. —*George Eliot*

Chapter 5

Coming of Age

Everyone wants to belong—whether it's to a family, church, or social club—and kids are no exception. But to fit in with any group, you need to do more than just show up. You have to study its history, understand its meaning, and be willing to assume the responsibilities that go along with membership. In the end, you go through an initiation rite. That's what this chapter's about: what to write for those coming-of-age celebrations when your children embrace their faith and heritage.

For Baptisms/Christenings

To some people it's a "baptism"; to others it's a "christening." Whatever you call it, it's a ceremony that introduces your baby into the Christian faith. It's also a chance for your family to welcome its newest member with a few special words.

To Parents

There's something refreshing about christenings. Babies add a sweet touch of reality to these solemn occasions. No matter what they do—laugh, cry, or spit up their food—we can't help but smile. Wishing you much love on your baby's special day.

Children's writer Kate Wiggins once said, "Every child born into the world is a new thought of God, an ever fresh and radiant possibility." What a remarkable feeling of hope and joy this day represents for you and your new son. May God continue to bless your family as you grow together.

To Babies

Today is your christening day. It's a day when God will hold you in his arms and shower you with hugs and kisses, just like your mommy and daddy. You're God's special little boy, and he'll love you forever. So will we!

Every time a new baby like you is born, God says, "Here's my gift to you, world." So treasure yourself and use your talents wisely because you're more than just you—you're a gift from God. That's why we love you so much.

The Write Way _____

Most people write to parents, but it's okay to send your note to a child. It can be kept in an album the baptized child can read when she's older. Imagine her pleasure, learning how people felt about her when she was an infant.

To Grandchildren

You are so dear to us, Tara, and we're excited to celebrate your christening with you. Please share this quote with your mom and dad. It's our hope for your new little family. "May they who love you be like the sun when it rises in its strength." (Judges 5:31) God bless you, sweetheart.

The day you were born we were overjoyed! Now we're looking forward to your baptism. Soon you'll be saying your first words and taking your first steps. There are so many "firsts" in a baby's life and so many ways to celebrate our love for you!

To Godchildren

I'm your godmother, Sara, and I love you. It's my job to help you grow up knowing God's love, too. You see, God loves all of us. That's why I'm here to celebrate your baptism. It's the day God says, "I love you, Sara. Welcome to the world."

When your parents asked me to be your godfather, I was afraid at first. I don't know much about babies, and I wasn't sure I could do the job. And then I saw your face. You looked up at me with such trust, I knew I had to say yes. You can count on me, Danny. I'll always be here for you.

To Nieces/Nephews

Hi there! I'm your Aunt Cissy—the one who makes funny faces. You won't understand until you're older, but baptisms are very important. When the priest pours water over you, it's God's way of making you *his* child, too. He can't resist you any more than we can. Wishing you tons of love always!

Hi champ! We've only met a few times, and you always scream when I pick you up. Let's hope we hit it off better when you get older. Meanwhile, here's a word of advice about baptism: wear the white dress and be a man about it. And try not to scream when they splash water on your head.

P.S. Uncle Art loves you.

To Older Children, Teens, and Adults

Being baptized when you're a little older makes the day more special to you, because you're grown up enough to understand what being a good Christian means. God bless you, honey, on this special day and for the rest of your life.

You're being baptized! I feel honored to be part of the congregation on your special day. You've always been the epitome of a good Christian, but today, you made it official. God bless you today and every day.

For First Communions

The next step—if you're 7 or 8 and have studied your catechism—is First Communion. It's a Roman Catholic rite that some Protestants celebrate. Girls wear a white dress with a veil (like a bride), and boys wear white pants and shirt, often with a clip-on bow tie (their first). To know what to write to the little tykes, read on.

To Sons/Daughters

A First Communion is an important time, Rosie. You've worked hard to learn about God, and now you can receive him like the rest of us. You must be very excited. Daddy and I are proud of how grown up you are today.

Since the day you were born, Mommy and I prayed that God would help us take care of you. He never let us down, and he won't let you down either. We are proud of all the work you did to get to this big day. We hope you are proud, too. God bless you, Tommy, on your First Communion.

> **The Write Way** _____
>
> Keep your notes to young children easy to read, and don't use "big words" they might not understand. Write about the importance of the ceremony and how they feel. Whatever you do, don't forget to praise them for their accomplishment.

To Grandchildren

Grandpa and I have such pride in you today. As you walk to the altar to receive your First Communion, be happy. God is your friend and helper. When you have a problem, just do what we do—pray—and you'll find an answer. We promise.

A long time ago, your Grandma and Grandpa had their First Communions, too. We were very excited, and our parents—your great-grandparents—were proud of us. Just like we are proud of you today. God bless you, David, on this special, holy day.

To Godchildren

Congratulations to my beautiful goddaughter. Now you are ready to receive Christ. It is a big step, but you are old enough and smart enough to take it. I hope your First Communion is a happy day for you.

Being your godfather is a great honor. It means your mom and dad think I am a good person who can help them look after you. I hope your First Communion is as special as mine was. You are a wonderful little girl, and you make me proud.

To Nieces/Nephews

You must be feeling very grown up today. You get to dress up and walk to the altar to receive your First Communion. We are all so happy for you. Congratulations to a very special niece!

> ### ✉ Greeting Goofs _____
>
> Don't hesitate to write about God and religion for coming-of-age celebrations. Faith is an important factor in these rites. In fact, you won't find too many cards that *aren't* religious. If you're not a believer, now is *not* the time to let people know.

God smiles down on all his children, all the time, every day. But on your First Communion day, his smile is even brighter. So is mine. Congratulations to my very grown-up nephew on his First Communion.

For Confirmations

Confirmation is an important step for Roman Catholics around the age of 13 and for some Protestants in their teens. When young Christians confirm, they're accepting responsibility for the promises their parents made for them at baptism. Such a grown-up commitment deserves a personal note, don't you think?

To Sons/Daughters

You did it! After all your studying and questions, you're ready to make a commitment to the Church. Mom and I are pleased with what you've accomplished. When we look at you now, we see a courageous boy on the threshold of becoming an exceptional man. We're proud to call you our son!

You're being confirmed—that means you're on the brink of adulthood. We're so proud. But as you grow and accept more responsibility, remember this: no matter what your age, you're still a child of God. We hope you confirm your love for him daily by continuing to be the wonderful, caring person you are.

To Grandchildren

Grandma and I are so thrilled. We were there for your baptism and your First Communion. And now for your Confirmation! You're officially on the road to adulthood. We pray that God's love will fill your heart and his wisdom will guide you, today and always. Congratulations!

The Write Way _____

Praise your youngsters for their achievements, and emphasize the responsibility they've taken on. You can also compliment them on how much they've grown.

Confirmation means you've strengthened and confirmed your faith in God. But God has always had a strong faith in you, just as we have. As you walk through life, remember to check for his footprints in the sand beside you. Congratulations to our grown-up grandson.

To Godchildren

You know what I've always loved about you? You're so natural in your relationship with God. For you, it's an everyday thing, not something you save for church on Sunday. You're kind, friendly, thoughtful, and generous—just what a soldier for Christ should be. Congratulations on making the grade!

When you were baptized, you were too little to know what joining Christ's Church meant. Now, God is calling you to affirm your faith publicly and asking you to make a lifelong commitment. I know you're ready. May you meet all of life's challenges knowing that God's grace and love will see you through.

To Nieces/Nephews

Do you know what it means "to confirm"? It means to strengthen. Not your muscles (I know you like to work out), but your faith. It's not easy to be a Christian. You're expected to live your faith, love it, and stand by it. I have a feeling you're up to the challenge! Congratulations to a special nephew.

"God is with you in all that you do." (Genesis 2:22) We can't always be there to protect you and guide you, but God can. Best wishes to my favorite niece on her Confirmation.

From Sponsors

I have one wish for you today. It's from a prayer by Saint Richard of Chichester, which inspired a song in *Godspell:* "May I know thee more clearly, love thee more dearly, follow thee more nearly, day by day." Congratulations on your Confirmation.

Today you're committing yourself to the Church for the first time. You've struggled to understand your faith and are ready to become a true soldier of Christ. As your sponsor, I'm proud of your achievement, and I promise always to stand by you.

Bar and Bat Mitzvahs

After studying their religion, Hebrew, and the Torah; learning how to lead a service; and volunteering (whew!), Jewish youngsters are ready to become adult members of the synagogue. Boys have bar mitzvahs at 13, and girls celebrate bat mitzvahs at 12. Here are some words of praise to celebrate their hard work.

To Sons/Daughters

We're so proud of you today. You've become a true son of the commandments. We also share in your happiness as you take this step forward in life. May the teachings of the Torah guide you on your journey. Mazel tov with love.

The Write Way

"Mazel tov" is another way of saying "congratulations" or "good luck" in Yiddish. It's usually reserved for special occasions—like a bar or bat mitzvah!

This is your day to shine! In our eyes you're a woman today, a daughter of the commandments. We pray that the Torah's teachings will guide you toward wisdom and faith as you walk through life. Congratulations on your bat mitzvah!

To Grandchildren

You've always been a blessing to us. Today—as you are called to the Torah—you are a double blessing. We pray that God's law will fill your heart with wisdom and lead you to a life of faith and happiness. Mazel tov!

What do you feel today? Pride, joy, a sense of accomplishment? You should feel all these and more. A short time ago you were a child. Today you are a woman in the eyes of God and our people. Mazel tov! May the memories of your bat mitzvah live with you always.

To Nieces/Nephews

Congratulations on your bat mitzvah. An old Jewish proverb tells us, "Do not be wise in words—be wise in deeds." The Torah has given you wisdom, but you must act on what you've learned. May its teachings always guide you toward your goals. Mazel tov to a special niece.

You've always been a source of pride to your family and friends, today more than ever. That's why we've come to witness your bar mitzvah— your entrance to adulthood. Study the Torah and you'll never lose sight of your faith. Mazel tov to a wonderful nephew.

For La Quinceañera

A Latina girl celebrates her passage to womanhood on her 15th birthday— it's called La Quinceañera. The day begins with a special Mass at which she commits herself to her faith and family. Here are some encouraging words you can write.

To Daughters

You're not our little girl anymore. Today you're a beautiful woman— ready for the challenges of life, family, and faith. We hope your journey will be blessed with all the joy and happiness you've given us. Happy 15th birthday.

You look like a princess today, with your sparkling tiara and beautiful gown. And even princesses need to remember to have faith in God and themselves. Congratulations, and save the first dance for me, Princess.

To Granddaughters

Happy birthday to my beautiful Quinceañera. Do you know how loved you are, dear granddaughter? From the day you were born you brought sunshine and laughter into our life. May God bless you on this special day, and may all your dreams come true.

God was good to us, allowing you to come into our lives 15 years ago. That's why I'm giving you this prayer book—to keep God's word in your life. Happy birthday to a granddaughter who is loved deeply.

The Write Way _____

People bring gifts to most coming-of-age ceremonies. Try writing about your gift in the note, particularly if it's a traditional gift with a special meaning for the day.

To Goddaughters

My gift to you is this beautiful tiara. As your godmother, I'll be crowning you with it at your Quinceañera celebration. It's a sign that you're a princess before God and the world. May it be a loving reminder of your special day. Happy birthday.

I'm delighted you asked me to be godmother at your Quinceañera. It makes me feel even closer to you. I hope your celebration is filled with special moments you can carry in your heart (and your photo album). Happy 15th birthday.

To Nieces

Girl! You're a woman now! When you switch your comfy flats for high heels, you'll really feel it! Seriously, have a wonderful time at your party. You're 15 today, and it's all about you. Happy birthday and enjoy the attention. You deserve it!

Greeting Goofs _____

Families love to tease, but be cautious about hurting someone's feelings, especially teenagers. If you must tease, do it in a light-hearted way and finish your note with something positive.

I hear my favorite niece—the one who wears torn jeans and sneakers all the time—is putting on a gown and heels for her Quinceañera! Looks like someone's growing up! You're going to look great, but do me a favor—don't lose the *kid* part of you completely. It's what I love the most. Happy birthday, kid!

From Friends to Friends

How cool is this? You get to dress like a princess with 14 boys and girls in your court, you get a fancy party, and you get tons of presents—just because you're 15! My turn next month!

I'm so excited about your Quinceañera, I can hardly stand it! You're gonna look great! And all those guys in tuxedoes—it's just like prom! Can you believe it? I'm speechless. Oh, yeah—happy birthday!

Quotes to Inspire You

Let the children come to me, do not hinder them; for to such belongs the kingdom of God. —*Mark 10:14*

Whoever follows me will never walk in darkness but will have the light of life. —*John 8:11*

It's faith in something and enthusiasm for something that makes a life worth living. —*Oliver Wendell Holmes*

Relying on God has to begin all over again every day as if nothing yet had been done. —*C. S. Lewis*

Faith is the strength by which a shattered world shall emerge into the light. —*Helen Keller*

God enters by a private door into every individual. —*Ralph Waldo Emerson*

It's not how much or how little you have that makes you great or small, but how much or how little you are with what you have. —*Rabbi Samson Raphael Hirsch*

If you want to be respected, you must respect yourself. —*Spanish proverb*

Chapter 6

Graduations

It's springtime, and the halls of academia are echoing with the stately sounds of "Pomp and Circumstance." Students are boasting about their achievements on the one hand and worrying about what comes next on the other. Meanwhile, Mom and Dad are still trying to figure out where the years went! Although 60 percent of graduation cards are bought for high school graduates, nowadays you'll find caps and gowns on everyone from preschool to premed. No doubt congratulations are in order, but what do you say? Age and relationship make all the difference.

Proud at Any Age

We love graduations. Everybody has them. Even kids in preschool march down the aisle to pick up their certificates of success. From the "very young" to the "not so young anymore," here are samples of what you can write to your favorite graduate.

For Preschool and Kindergarten Graduation

You graduated from preschool today. Good job! You know what comes next? Lots of hugs and kisses from Mommy and Daddy. We love our smart "big" girl.

Happy graduation, big guy! You aced kindergarten, and do you know what comes next? Ready, set, go … to first grade!

For Elementary School Graduation

You are a genius. You graduated from elementary school, and your grades in math and science are out of this world! Can't wait to see what a few years in middle school will do for you. You're on your way to the stars, girl!

Congrats, graduate! They threw finger painting, long division, and spelling bees at you and you passed with flying colors. Here's to middle school and all new challenges.

For Middle School Graduation

We interrupt this card for a special report: the word is out. Gary Hopkins is graduating from middle school! Yes, folks, Gary is officially ready for high school. The real question? Is high school ready for Gary! Way to go, and knock 'em dead!

First you conquered elementary school, now you've tackled middle school. Kid, you're on a roll. Congratulations. With your track record, high school should be a breeze.

For High School Graduation

You did it! You really did it! High school's not easy, but you pulled it off. I always knew you were smart, talented, and witty. Now you're educated, too! High five, grad! (You can count to five, can't you?)

"The fireworks begin today. Each diploma is a lighted match. Each one of you is a fuse." Edward Koch, former mayor of New York City, said that. College is a time of discovery. Find something that lights your fire and go for it!

The Write Way _____

Praise your graduate for something she's achieved. If she won a sports trophy or a special music award, mention it in your note. It shows that you're paying attention.

For College Graduation

I know your brain is crammed with four years of college courses, but here's an excerpt from Life 101: balance your checkbook, don't wash red clothes with white ones, and change the oil in your car every 3,000 miles. Oh, and I almost forgot—ignore everyone's advice and follow your dreams!

Greeting Goofs _____

Planning on offering "helpful hints" to a graduate? Be sure the graduate is open to them first, because advice isn't always welcome. Be tactful or find a quote that expresses what you want to say.

Broadcast journalist David Frost said, "Don't aim for success if you want it; just do what you love and believe in, and it will come naturally." I'm so glad you followed your heart and majored in education. Here's to your brilliant teaching career! I envy your future students!

For Nursing School Graduation

Congratulations! You're officially an R.N. I hear that's nursing lingo for "registered nurse." I can't imagine anyone better for the job. You're warm and friendly, and you enjoy helping people. Anyone who finds you in his hospital room is one lucky guy—or gal!

The British soldiers during the Crimean War called Florence Nightingale "the lady with the lamp" because she visited patients in the middle of the night. See—I did my research. You obviously did yours, too, graduating from nursing school with honors. Here's to our own Florence Nightingale!

Greeting Goofs

Don't make negative comments like "college is tough" or "jobs are impossible to find these days." Most grads have no illusions about the problems they're facing. Pointing it out only adds to their apprehension.

For an Advanced Degree

We were beginning to think you were a permanent student. But you fooled us all by getting your Ph.D. in English *and* history. What an accomplishment! You actually must have been studying all that time! (And here I was convinced you were goofing around.) Congrats, Doc!

Most people are satisfied with high school and college degrees, but you had to be different. Congratulations to our favorite overachiever. May your thirst for knowledge never be quenched. We're very proud of you!

For Trade School Graduation

The word's out! You got a diploma in automotive technology. I recall that '67 Chevy you worked on in high school. You had that baby purring like a kitten. I hope you're looking for a job around here. We could use a good mechanic, and you fit the bill!

Remember how we used to put on your mom's lipstick and play movie stars? You always had a flair for fashion and makeup, and now that you've graduated from beauty school, you can help the rest of us look stunning, too. Congratulations to one of the beautiful people!

Greeting Goofs

Avoid criticism—even if your graduate's in the bottom of the class. Be grateful she's graduating, and say something positive about her personality or talents. This is a time to celebrate.

For Police Academy Graduation

When you were accepted as a recruit in the police academy, we were thrilled. And after months of rigorous training, we see a big difference in you. We knew you had good moral character, but now you also have the strength and confidence of a leader. Congratulations on your graduation!

Most people watch TV cop shows for fun. Who knew you were laying the groundwork for your future? Here's to a long and rewarding career in law enforcement. We can't think of anyone more dedicated to the cause or more qualified to protect the public!

The Write Way

Write about the values you admire in your recipient such as courage, integrity, and respect. Let him know you're proud of him and excited about his future.

For Military Graduation

We're so proud you've graduated from Army basic training—and with an Honor Graduate ribbon! Could you hear us cheering when you went up to receive your certificate from the commander? We never imagined our daughter would be so courageous!

Having a son graduate from Annapolis—we're so proud! On graduation day, you looked so handsome in your uniform and so serious about the commitment you were making. Not many parents can boast their son is helping to make the world a safer place. But we can—and we are! You're our hero, and we love you.

It's All Relative

Your daughter graduated from high school, your nephew got his certificate from a culinary institute, and Grandma got her B.A. in physical education. All good reasons to celebrate, and here's how to do it.

To Sons/Daughters

We're so pleased with what you've accomplished in the past four years of high school. You worked hard in class and on the sports field. Your friends and coaches love you. You're a real people person. Congratulations. We are so proud to have you as our daughter.

Humorist Erma Bombeck said, "Graduation day is tough for adults. They go to the ceremony as parents. They come home as contemporaries. After twenty-two years of child-raising, they are unemployed." Congratulations, son. We're happy and proud to be standing in the unemployed parents' line.

To Grandchildren

We've always thought you were a winner, and now the rest of the world knows, too. Congratulations on all your hard work and achievements. You make us proud, graduate!

My house is filled with photos of you, and now I can't wait to add your graduation picture to my collection. Best wishes to my wonderful, handsome grandson on graduating from high school and being accepted at college. I might run out of space for your pictures, but I'll never run out of space for you in my heart!

To Brothers/Sisters

Rumor has it my baby brother graduated from high school. For real? The little runt who still reads comic books and collects *Star Wars* action figures? (Ah, the secrets a big sister knows.) Way to go, Luke Skywalker! I'm proud of you.

The Write Way

Personalize your notes by making a connection between the past and the present. Maybe your niece was a budding scientist who collected bugs or your nephew in the police academy played cops and robbers.

Hey big sister! You're actually graduating from college? I thought for sure you'd flunk out or take 6 years to finish. Seriously, I'm proud of you, I miss you, and I can't wait to see what you do next in life. After all, I'll be following in your footsteps ....

To Nieces/Nephews

When you were two, you loved to construct little buildings with your blocks. Now you're finishing college with an architecture degree and going to graduate school. Who knew you were on your way all those years ago? Congratulations! You're a natural!

Remember when you were little and we baked cookies together? I'll never forget how hard you concentrated while your little hands shaped the dough. Even then you had a gift for baking! Now you're graduating from culinary arts college. I'm so proud of you and so happy I had a hand in shaping a future pastry chef!

To Friends

Good-bye. Farewell. So long. See ya. Adios. Hasta la vista, baby. Guess that about covers it. You graduated and you're moving away …. Congratulations and good for you! Sure I'll miss you, but we can still e-mail and call, and I'll come and visit! Here's to us—friends forever!

Someone once wrote, "It's really amazing when two strangers become the best of friends, but it's really sad when the best of friends become two strangers." No way that's happening to us. So what if you graduated and moved away—it just gives me someplace new to visit! Best wishes, best friend!

To Boyfriends/Girlfriends

You know how they say that graduation is an end and a beginning? Well, I sure hope it is—an end to all your studying and a beginning of our time with each other for a change. Honey, you know I'm really proud of you. Now what about getting a job so you can take care of me in style!

"Try not to become a man of success, but rather try to become a man of value." Albert Einstein said that. You know, the $E = mc^2$ guy. Here's a graduation equation I just made up: you + me = 1 great team. Stick with me, baby, and we'll have success *and* value!

To Fellow Graduates

We've been through hell and back, but we did it! All those late nights— guzzling coffee, writing papers, studying for exams. Know what I think? "The tassel's worth the hassle!" I don't know who said it but I love it. Congrats to my favorite co-grad!

We finally made it! Can't say I'll miss the all-nighters, cafeteria food, or early classes, but I sure will miss you! You were the *best* roomie—it was pure luck they put us together freshman year! Hope our luck holds out with future roommates—and with our future lives. Best of luck to my best friend!

Graduation Asides

Other people need to be applauded for graduations—teachers and parents, for starters. Also the student who goes to school later in life. And what about religious professionals? Don't they work just as hard to reach their goals? Here are some thoughts.

To Teachers

I'm so grateful for all you did for me. You weren't always my favorite person (I'm thinking of the long homework assignments), but you taught me to think for myself and not take the easy way out. I'll never forget what I learned this year. Thanks for the knowledge.

The Write Way

Advice for graduates: a note to your teachers or parents is always welcome and will mean a lot to them. Let them know you appreciate their support. Make it personal by mentioning at least one way they helped.

Thank you for being my teacher, my mentor, and my friend. You believed in me when other people didn't and encouraged me to apply to the theater arts program at City College. I can't believe I got accepted. I'm still pinching myself! Thank you so much. I promise to send you free tickets when I get to Broadway!

To Parents

I know you're supposed to be congratulating me today, but I think you folks deserve some credit. Without your support (both emotional and financial), I couldn't have made it. You've always been there for me, and I hope I can do the same for you some day. Congratulations to two amazing parents!

It's me, your daughter—the cute, quirky nonconformist? I'm putting a new spin on graduation wishes by saying "Thank you for helping me through everything from potty training to driver training with love, patience, and humor." Now I'm off to college, and I owe it all to you! I love you guys!

To Older Graduates

How did you do it? Raising kids while going to college should earn you more than just a degree. You should get a Medal of Honor! Your kids must be so proud. I know I am. Congratulations, graduate!

Congratulations on earning a college degree in physical education, Grandma! No big surprise there. You taught me to swim, played catch with me, and led the way down the mountain at the ski slopes. I used to brag to my friends that I had the coolest grandma—and I still do! Here's to your brilliant career!

For Ordinations

Congratulations on your new ministry. May God's love be with you as you celebrate the mysteries of Christ and serve his people. You are always in our prayers—especially today.

As you go into the world to serve God, may this quote from St. Vincent de Paul guide you: "If God is the center of your life, no words are necessary. Your mere presence will touch hearts." You've already touched our hearts forever. Congratulations on your ordination.

For Religious Vows

You have chosen to serve God as your life work. May he bless you on your special day of consecration, and may our prayerful good wishes be with you always.

Mother Teresa once said, "I am a little pencil in the hand of a writing God who is sending a love letter to the world." I think God has found another little pencil—you. May your love make as much difference in the world as Mother Teresa's. Blessings on this special day as you consecrate yourself to God.

Graduation Blessings

Graduations tend to inspire us. If God and inspiration are your cup of tea, sharing those thoughts with others is fine—as long as you know they will welcome them.

Religious

Congratulations! You've graduated! Eleanor Powell, a famous film actress and dancer in the 1930s and 1940s, said, "What we are is God's gift to us. What we become is our gift to God." What you've become is an amazing gift to God. Keep up the good work!

I came across a quote from an unknown author: "God gives us dreams a size too big so that we can grow into them." I hope you'll have tons of super-size dreams and never stop growing into them. We're proud of you.

> **The Write Way** _____
>
> A religious message makes sense for a baptism or church wedding, but think twice before sending one for a nonreligious occasion. Even if you know the recipient is a churchgoer, play it safe by using quotes like the ones shown here.

Spiritual

As you graduate from high school and decide what to do with your life, maybe this quote from Buddha will help: "Your work is to discover your world and then with all your heart give yourself to it." Discover, give, enjoy. Happy graduation.

This quote comes from Paul Taylor, an Australian aborigine: "We are all given a song line. That's what you are meant to do with your life. When you do that, it makes you happy and it makes everything happy around you." Congratulations, and follow your song line all the way to happiness.

Quotes to Inspire You

Do not follow where the path may lead. Go, instead, where there is no path and leave a trail. —_Ralph Waldo Emerson_

Be who you are and say what you feel, because those who mind don't matter and those who matter don't mind. —_Dr. Seuss_

Shoot for the moon. Even if you miss, you'll land among the stars. —_Les Brown, motivational speaker_

It is not the mountain we conquer but ourselves. —_Edmund Hillary_

Don't live down to expectations. Go out there and do something remarkable. —_Wendy Wasserstein, playwright_

Dream as if you'll live forever. Live as if you'll die today. —_James Dean_

Love your life, perfect your life, beautify all things in your life.
Seek to make your life long, and its purpose in the service of your
people. —*Chief Tecumseh*

To those of you who received honors, awards and distinctions, I say well
done. And to the C students, I say you too may one day be president of
the United States. —*President George W. Bush*

Put your future in good hands—your own. —*Unknown*

Chapter 7

Shining Moments

"Well done!" "You're the best!" "We knew you could do it!"
Who doesn't enjoy a word or two of praise after achieving
a goal? From your baby's first step to the day you retire, a
pat on the back is always welcome. Was your wife promoted
to manager? Did your nephew get his driver's license? Did
Grandma win a blue ribbon for growing the best tomatoes in
the county? Why not help celebrate their accomplishment by
sending a card with a personal message of congratulations?

On the Job

*Here's to the workers who rise above the crowd and make a name for
themselves, whether it's salesman of the year or partner in a company.
For such accomplishments, kudos like the following will be welcome.*

For Good Salesmanship

You're salesman of the year! Congratulations! We're sending you
a bottle of champagne to help you celebrate. Good luck from the
second and third best salesmen of the year!

We always said you could sell sand in the Sahara, and this proves it! Congratulations on your salesmanship award. You work hard and it shows.

For Promotions

You got promoted to manager after only two years! That's quite an achievement. Your boss must admire your organizational and people skills. They sure come in handy at home. Way to go, Mom! I'm proud of you!

> **Greeting Goofs** _____
>
> Don't make someone search for a compliment; mention the good news up front. And don't forget to offer your congratulations. Let him know you're excited about his or her victory.

Another promotion? Fantastic! Pretty soon you'll be running the company. Just don't forget us little people as you're climbing the ladder of success. Congratulations from your downwardly mobile friends.

For Partnerships

What terrific news! No one deserves to be made partner more than you. You've given so much to the company for the past few years, how could they *not* make you partner? You have a bright future ahead of you. Congratulations!

I hear you made partner. You know a quality I've always admired about you? Your honesty. I'm sure your clients appreciate that their business affairs are in safe hands. Your colleagues must, too, or they wouldn't have given you this promotion. Congratulations and best wishes for a successful future.

For Starting a Business

Congratulations on opening your own hair salon. You've worked hard for this day and you finally made it happen. I've always said no one cuts my hair the way you do. How soon can I get an appointment?

You're leaving the ad agency to write at home? Do you actually think you can concentrate without people gossiping in the next cubicle, phones ringing off the hook, and memos and meetings all day long? Hmmm ... do you need an assistant? Best of luck!

For Retirements

I just heard the news that you're retiring. You'll be missed, but I'm happy for you. It's time to fulfill all those promises you've made to yourself for years, like fishing on weekdays when everyone else is at work. Let's also promise to stay friends. Best wishes for a more relaxed future. See you on the water!

Retiring? That can't be—you're only about 35, aren't you? What's your secret? Botox? Yoga? Green tea? Or maybe you just know how to set priorities and enjoy life. Here's to many happy and productive years ahead. Enjoy, enjoy, enjoy!

The Write Way

Share your confidence about a person's future success. Let her know how much you admire and respect her and that you will continue to be a support for her.

Stepping It Up

We set goals for ourselves all the time, some out of necessity—like potty training or a driver's license—and others for the challenge—like running for office. Keep reading for examples of what to say in different situations.

For Potty Training

You did it! No more diapers! It's big boy pants for you. We are so proud. Here is a present from Grandma and Grandpa. Quarters for your piggy bank! Hooray!

Greeting Goofs

Don't underestimate a child's need to be congratulated. Success at potty training might not mean much to you, but it means a lot to a toddler—and his parents! Let them know you're proud.

You're using the potty now! Good for you. It was sort of scary at first, but you figured it out because you're a smart, big girl. We're so proud of you, we're going to cheer and jump up and down. Yaaaaay!

For Passing a Test

You've been sweating these SAT exams for a year now. I told you not to worry, and wasn't I right? You got a great score because you're a genius! Any college would be thrilled to accept you, so relax and start applying, genius.

You passed the bar exam! Talk about an accomplishment! Now that you're licensed to practice law in this state, we see a rewarding, challenging career in your future. Congratulations! You're the #1 lawyer in our book—bar none!

The Write Way _____

Describe the person's achievement. Write about his strengths or the values he embodies that helped him achieve his goal. And above all, let him know you're proud.

For Getting a Driver's License

You got your driver's license? Awesome. Now you have to get Mom and Dad to pay for the insurance! You could get a job, but then you wouldn't have time to drive me around! Good job, bro.

You got your license on the first try! You'll be surprised to learn I flunked the first time. Oh, you aren't surprised? Okay, wise guy—here are the car keys and a grocery list. Pick up the dry cleaning while you're at it. Hey, you need the practice!

P.S. Dad and I are proud of you—just be careful!

For Acceptance to School

Congratulations! You're off to college! Sounds like they want you as much as we do—if that's possible. We'll miss you more than you can know. I hope this little gift of a phone card will inspire you to keep in touch. Love, Mom.

You got your letter of acceptance from Penn State? I can't wait to tell my friends! I'm as excited as if I were going there myself. In fact, I have every intention of reliving my college years through you, so you'd better e-mail your grandma once a week and send pictures! I love you, and I'm so proud of you.

For Becoming a Citizen

Congratulations! You're a naturalized citizen. I speak for all our fellow citizens when I say we're so pleased to have you join the melting pot!

We were thrilled to hear you're becoming a naturalized citizen. You've worked long and hard to join our beautiful country. Our thoughts and best wishes are with you as you celebrate.

For Election to Office

Congratulations! You won in a landslide. We couldn't be happier for you. We're especially thrilled that an honest and dedicated woman like you will represent us in the state legislature. Give our regards to the governor.

> **Greeting Goofs**
>
> Don't overdo the compliments or lavish someone with extravagant praise because you'll only sound insincere. Be straightforward and personal. A simple "Congratulations" can go a long way.

Just heard the news; you're the new president of the neighborhood housing association. The group will benefit from your organizational skills as well as your ability to remain calm in the face of a storm. Have a fabulous year!

And the Award Goes to ...

Those pop-ups on the Internet are always congratulating you for being the zillionth person to log on. But real people win real awards for real victories every day. Here are some words to express your congratulations when the success is genuine.

For School Awards

We're so proud you've been asked to join the National Honor Society. Your good grades definitely had something to do with it, but we're sure it's your volunteer work at the nursing home that caught their attention. We love the compassionate young woman you've become. Congratulations.

Class president, huh? Obviously, you're a young woman who isn't afraid of competition. Keep your eye on the goal, and you could be the future junior senator from New York—maybe even the first woman president of the United States! You've got my vote, girl!

For Sports Awards

I hear you're the most outstanding girls' basketball player in the district! Doesn't surprise me. You're an amazing athlete—on an amazing team— and a model of good sportsmanship. See you at the banquet, winner!

How about that—golf coach of the year for the third year in a row? You must be proud, yet I've never heard you brag. At least, not about your own achievements. But you never spare the praise for the kids on your team. In my book, that makes you a winner. Way to go, Coach!

For Community Awards

I saw your picture in the paper as the recipient of the town's community service award. Planning and organizing a communal garden in the lot next to the school is quite an achievement. And getting the students to help was a stroke of genius. What would our town do without you? Congratulations (and thank you)!

I just heard you were elected Businesswoman of the Year. What great news! I can't think of anyone who deserves the award more. For five years you've worked hard to make Flowers by Francesca a success, and it's paid off! Your customers love you, and obviously so do the other shop owners. Good for you!

For Artistic Awards

Congratulations on your NEPTA award for best actress in a drama. I'm surprised it took so long for them to honor you. You always put on a terrific show—onstage and off. You've been a winner in my book for years. Brava!

How do you do it? I can hardly draw a straight line, and you're winning awards for your watercolor landscapes! I'm so in awe of the time, effort, and talent you put into creating a fine work of art. I plan to be at your next show—with my checkbook!

For Professional Awards

I just heard about your recent award for Distinction in Research from Tulane University. You must be thrilled that your work in gene therapy for primates is finally being recognized. I'm not only happy for you, I'm proud to be your friend.

Extra, extra, read all about it! I just heard the news: you won first place in the Keystone Press Awards for your story on the impact of hunting on the economy of Pike County. Today *Keystone Press*, tomorrow, the Pulitzer prize!

It Was Tough, but I Did It

When accomplishing your goal means putting your nose to the grindstone or facing your demons, it makes the reward all the sweeter. Here are some words for those who succeeded in toughing it out.

For Recitals

Last night a star was born! After years of dance school and hours of practice, you weren't my niece anymore—you were a dancer! And sensational! How can you get up on your tippy toes like that and still look so graceful? Put me down for tickets the next time you perform. I wouldn't miss it for the world.

When you sat down at the piano, it was magic. Your rendition of "Moonlight Sonata" was breathtaking, from the opening notes to the finale. You were the shining star at the recital, honey. Encore, encore!

For Completing a Marathon

You did it! You ran the marathon and made it to the end. Ever hear this quote before? "Life's problems wouldn't be called 'hurdles' if there wasn't a way to get over them." You got over your hurdles all right, and you did it in style. I couldn't be prouder.

The Write Way _____

Acknowledge any difficulties someone had in achieving a goal. And don't underestimate the power of praise. A few positive words may be just what someone needs to keep going.

You're amazing. Only a year ago you were struggling to lose weight and trying to stick to an exercise program. Now you've finished your first marathon! Just thinking about running 26 miles makes me hit the wall. Keep on running, sister. You're my hero!

For Making a Speech

You know what they say—practice makes perfect. You must have practiced hard because your speech was perfect. You were fantastic and the crowd loved you. What a great job!

The Write Way

What a great opportunity to add an inspirational quote! Choose one of the quotes at the end of this chapter or look on the web. Appendix B at the end of the book can tell you where to go.

I read somewhere that the average American is more afraid of public speaking than of death. Well, you're obviously way above average because you had the audience in the palm of your hand tonight. A toast to my speechmaking friend—you knocked 'em dead!

For Getting Something Published

How exciting! They published your paper on early modern English history. It's amazing how you can make history come alive. Did I hear correctly about a book in the works? You're such a terrific writer. Here's hoping it's a huge success. I can't wait to buy it!

I just read your article on acute chest pain in *Emergency Journal*, and it's excellent. I'm impressed that you can run a thriving cardiology practice and still find time to publish several times a year. Plus, you play a mean round of golf! Keep up the good work!

Accomplishment Blessings

Some people believe faith in God is what makes all our dreams possible. As long as you know your opinion is shared, you can say it like this in a note.

Religious

Congratulations on opening your third store. Martin Luther King Jr. said, "Faith is taking the first step even when you don't see the whole staircase." You didn't know where you were going, but you started the journey anyway. Now you have success beyond your wildest dreams. Best wishes to a woman with faith.

Someone once said, "Faith makes things possible, not easy." I know the past few months haven't been easy for you, but you've held strong to your commitment to stay away from drugs. That's because you had faith in God and in yourself. Congratulations on making it this far. I'm proud of what you've done.

Spiritual

I heard you won an award for starting a food bank in Madison. Congratulations! Native American chief Seattle said, "Take only memories, leave nothing but footprints." The footprints you're leaving are enormous. I hope others will be able to follow them.

Congratulations on your photography show. My favorite writer, Anne Lamott, said, "Hope begins in the dark, the stubborn hope that if you just show up and try to do the right thing, the dawn will come." You've been working at it for years and people, at last, are realizing what a talent you are. Welcome to the dawn!

Quotes to Inspire You

Excellence is not a skill. It is an attitude. —*Motivational speaker Ralph Marston*

If you aren't fired with enthusiasm, you will be fired with enthusiasm. —*Vince Lombardi*

You have to expect things of yourself before you can do them. —*Michael Jordan*

Things turn out best for the people who make the best out of the way things turn out. —*Art Linkletter*

Obstacles are those frightful things you see when you take your eyes off your goal. —*Henry Ford*

The will to win, the desire to succeed, the urge to reach your full potential … these are the keys that will unlock the door to personal excellence. —*Eddie Robinson*

If opportunity doesn't knock, build a door. —*Milton Berle*

Only those who dare to fail greatly can ever achieve greatly. —*Robert Francis Kennedy*

Chapter 8

Don't Forget to Say Thank You

There's nothing more frustrating than putting time and effort into giving someone the perfect gift—and then not getting a note of appreciation. Okay, so you loved the gift but you didn't get around to sending a thank you. "Silent gratitude isn't much use to anyone," said writer Gladys Stern. Shouldn't you do something about it? Let's give it a try: Aunt Hilda knits you a sweater for your birthday, your best friend gives you a place setting of china for your wedding, or the girls at work send a basketful of newborn clothes for your baby shower. All together now: what are you gonna do? Send a thank you note!

Thanks for Your Gift

From bridal showers to baby showers, people shower us with gifts each year. The rule is to send a note, even if you thank someone in person. Have you ever heard anyone complain about getting too many thank you notes? Here are some ways to show your gratitude.

For Engagement Parties

Thank you for the wedding countdown clock. We've set the date, and it's keeping us on schedule. What a perfect reminder of this special time. Only you could think of a gift so practical and yet so romantic.

What an original idea—a booklover's gift basket! You're obviously a true friend, because you picked the perfect gift for two homebodies like us. A vanilla-scented candle, a selection of herbal teas, biscotti, best-sellers, and the two of us snuggled on the couch. Can't wait! Thanks a million!

For Bridal Showers

Champagne flutes! And they're personalized with our names and the date of the wedding! Thank you. We'll think of you fondly when we drink from them on our wedding day.

Thank you so much for the beautiful engraved photo album. What a thoughtful—and practical—gift. We're already putting pictures in, starting with the ones from the bridal shower. Whenever we open the album, we'll think of you.

For Weddings

How thoughtful of you to give us an elegant crystal picture frame as a wedding gift. It's the perfect showcase for our wedding portrait. We can't wait for you to visit so you can see it in its place of honor on the mantel.

Greeting Goofs

Never send a preprinted thank you card. Handwrite your thank you's on a note card or personal stationery. For weddings or other formal events, use good-quality paper or engraved or printed stationery.

Matt and I were thrilled to receive the place setting of china from you. It's a gorgeous pattern, isn't it? We can't wait to have fancy dinner parties and use all our wedding gifts. We promise you and Hank will be among the first to sit at our table. Thank you again.

For Baby Showers

Tom and I would like to thank you for the mobile you gave us to put over the baby's crib. It plays Mozart and Beethoven—two of my favorites. Imagine falling asleep and waking up to the classics while cute little animals dance above your head. What a lucky baby!

Thank you so much for the baby towels and wash cloths. They're so tiny and soft—just like our baby will be! I love the way the towels have hoods to keep little heads warm. What a wonderful, useful gift from our friend who obviously knows her way around babies. Thanks again.

For Births and Adoptions

I can't thank you enough for the box of onesies you gave us when Emma was born. She wears them every day, alone or with one of her baby outfits. They come in so many colors, they match just about everything she has!

What a beautiful gift! An adoption life book that we can fill with pictures and memories for our little angel. I especially love the title, *I Am Chosen*. Thank you for choosing the perfect gift. We love it!

For Birthdays

How did you know I wanted an iPod shuffle? Not only did you get me *the* most perfect present ever, but you got it in the exact color I wanted. Thank you so much! I can't wait to start listening to it!

Thanks so much for the gift certificate from Macy's. It really fills the bill, not that I plan on applying it to my bill. No way—I'm going to shop till I drop! Care to join me?

For Anniversaries

Thank you for the exquisite porcelain vase you gave us as an anniversary gift. The hand-painted water lilies remind me of my favorite Monet painting. Brad and I will treasure it always.

The Write Way _____

Write soon after you receive a gift, and describe what you like about it. Let the giver know how the gift will be used or how it makes your life better.

The silver bowl is breathtaking, and having it engraved with our names and "Happy 25th Anniversary" added the perfect touch. It looks beautiful atop our dining room buffet. I plan to show it off in more practical ways, too, next time I make my English trifle. Dessert anyone?

For Coming-of-Age Moments

The baptismal bracelet you gave Lucy is charming. We love that the crystal is the color of her birthstone—amethyst—and that her name is spelled out in sterling silver blocks. The bracelet fits perfectly on her wrist, and she looks like a little princess when she's wearing it. Thank you.

Alison would like to thank you for the book of Bible stories you gave her for her First Communion. The story about Noah's Ark is her favorite. We read it every night, and Alison even made a drawing for you of Noah with all the animals. You couldn't have chosen a more perfect gift.

Thank you for my Confirmation gifts. I'm saving the money for my class trip, and I'm wearing the sterling silver cross to my 8th grade graduation. It's really beautiful—I love it.

Thank you for the book you gave me at my bar mitzvah. It was fun to read about kids growing up in Israel today. The Star of David bookmark was also cool. It will come in handy because I really like to read.

The necklace and earrings set you gave me for my Quinceañera is gorgeous. The baby blue stones matched my dress perfectly. Thank you for helping me feel so beautiful on my special day.

For Graduations

How can I thank you enough for your generous graduation gift? I'm using it to buy my college textbooks for first semester. If I'm careful, I may even have some left over for second semester. Your gift took a huge load off my mind. I'll never forget it.

A $100 phone card? What a great gift! I guess you're hinting that I should call you from college, and I promise I will. You know I love to e-mail, but I know you'd rather hear my voice instead. It'll be great to hear yours, too. Thanks again. Love ya.

When Leaving a Job

Thank you for the good-looking gold watch the group gave me for my retirement. It was so thoughtful of you. I plan to wear it to church and on special occasions. No need to wear it during the week. My time is my own from now on. (Sorry, couldn't resist.) You're a great bunch of people. I'll miss you.

The Write Way

When you receive a gift from a group of people, you should write individual thank you's. If it's from a group of co-workers or a club, one thank you (to be posted) is enough.

You couldn't have chosen a better gift for me than the leather portfolio. Now I have a classy container for my writing samples as I pound the pavement looking for freelance work. Every time I open the case, I'll think of you guys. I miss you already!

For Christmas

Thanks for the one-of-a-kind "fun fur" scarf you made me for Christmas. When did you learn to knit? It's my favorite color—lavender—and it matches my coat perfectly. I'm sending you a picture so you can see how great it looks on me. Thanks, sis.

> ### The Write Way
>
> Christmas is a great time to teach children how to write thank you notes. Let them help choose—or make!—the cards. A younger child might be able to sign his or her name to what you've written or draw a picture of the gift.

A gift certificate for a massage—I can't wait! You've heard me say I'd love to try one, but you knew I'd never spend the money on myself. Thank you so much for giving me permission to get pampered. I feel more relaxed already.

For Hanukkah

Thank you for the colorful plush menorah you sent Jacob as a Hanukkah gift. Each night he places his own plush "candle" in a branch of the menorah—just like the grown-ups. It makes him feel so important. What a wonderful way for him to learn about our traditions!

Many thanks for the tripod you sent as a Hanukkah gift. What a perfect choice for this time of year. I attached my camera right away. Now I can take all the family pictures I want—and be in them myself!

Thanks for Your Hospitality

Hospitality is another good reason to express your appreciation. Whether it's a dinner party or a weekend visit, show you are a grateful guest by sending your host or hostess a thank you note like one of these.

For Parties in Your Honor

What a cool surprise! A 30th birthday with all my old friends. And *you* made it happen! I can't believe I didn't see it coming. Everyone was there, and the gifts were amazing. You know what the best part was? You, girl. You're the best. Thanks!

Dad and I would like to thank you kids for the 35th anniversary party you had for us. It was such a treat to have the family all together again. You really shouldn't have done it—but we're glad you did! We had a wonderful time.

For Weekend Visits

Last weekend's visit to your country house was wonderful. You wined and dined us into the wee hours, and Bill spent the next day showing us the sights. I can't remember the last time I had so much fun. We'd love to return the favor by having you over for dinner. How about Thursday? Give me a call. And thanks!

There's nothing like a weekend at the beach with you and your family. The weather was perfect, the food was divine, and the company was excellent. The best part was lolling around on a sandy beach with occasional dips in the ocean to cool off. I have only one thing to say—thanks for a fabulous weekend!

The Write Way _____

When you thank someone for his or her hospitality, be specific about what you enjoyed. Also mention the other people present—especially family members—and show some enthusiasm!

Thanks for Your Support

You were in the hospital for surgery, or maybe you were sick at home and had to stay in bed. Everyone was so helpful with gifts, visits, and calls offering support or assistance. And the nurses at the hospital were angels. You have so many people to thank, don't you? Try some of these notes for starters.

For Gifts

How sweet of you to bring me all those murder mysteries while I was laid up in bed. They took my mind off my illness and made a lengthy recovery seem shorter. And I now have some new favorite authors to read. I can't thank you enough.

Your kind gift of flowers meant a lot to me when I was in the hospital. Any time I was depressed, I looked over at the smiley face mug filled with yellow roses and white daisies. It was impossible not to smile back. Thanks for cheering me up!

For Assistance

It's been a while since you drove me to the emergency room at Mercy Hospital. I'm happy to say that I now feel well enough to thank you for your quick thinking that afternoon. My situation could have become life-threatening, but thanks to you, I'm back to my old self again. You'll never know how grateful I am.

The Write Way _____

You don't have to send a thank you while you're sick, of course. But as soon as you are able, send a short note of gratitude for any gifts, support, or assistance you received.

I'm so thankful for your help during my illness. All those trips to the doctor's office took time out of your day, but you didn't complain. You made me feel like I was doing you a favor. Thanks for being such a gem.

For Hospital Visits

A hospital can be a boring place, but your frequent visits always cheered me up. It was nice to know that someone cared enough to come by so often. You're a dear friend, and I'll never forget your kindness. Thank you.

Thanks for coming to see me in the hospital. Between the IV and the daily blood drawing, I felt like a pincushion. But you helped me see the humor in it—even though it hurt to laugh! A friend like you was just what the doctor ordered.

For Emotional Support

What would I do without you? No matter how depressed I got from the treatment, you always convinced me I could handle it. Just holding your hand made me feel better. Thank you for being there for me.

They say you know who your real friends are when life gets tough. Going through surgery isn't a stroll in the park, but hearing your voice on the phone every day made me strong. Thank you for letting me know what a real friend is.

To Hospital Staff

Every day in every way, you're the most amazing group of people I've ever met. During my stay at Mercy Hospital, your patience and professionalism knew no bounds. This box of chocolates is my way of saying thank you. Enjoy!

The Write Way

It's a nice gesture to send a thank you note—and a small gift—to the staff at the hospital where you stayed, especially if your stay was extended or your loved one passed away there.

I can't say enough about the wonderful care I received while I was at Mt. Hope Hospital. You were all so patient and never lost your sense of humor, even though I was a little cranky at times. I'm sending you a bottle of champagne to celebrate my recovery—off-duty, of course. Think of it as my toast to you.

Thanks for Your Sympathy

When someone you love dies, the support you get from the people around you means everything. Believe it or not, taking the time to thank people for their kindness can help the healing process. If you don't feel up to doing it yourself, ask a member of your family to do it for you. Here are some thoughts on what to say.

For Cards and Flowers

Your touching note about your friendship with Jane brought me to tears. They were good tears, however, knowing that you and she shared so many wonderful times together. When you lose someone you love, you sometimes forget that other people are losing someone, too. Thank you for sharing your love with me.

The Write Way _____

It isn't necessary to send a thank you for every sympathy card you receive. Only do so if someone added a personal note to the card or sent a Mass card, which requires a small donation.

Thank you for the lovely spray of snapdragons, white carnations, and daisies you and Uncle Vic sent when Mother passed away. You know how much she would have loved them. Your presence at the funeral was also comforting. Thank you for being there.

For Acts of Kindness

I can't thank you enough for all your help after my brother's sudden death. The many trips you made to the airport to pick up our friends and relatives will not be forgotten. You're a true friend.

The Write Way _____

When you're dealing with the death of a loved one, writing a thank you note might be the last thing on your mind. Take advantage of the preprinted cards the funeral home probably provides, and just add a brief personal note.

Thank you so much for inviting my aunt and uncle to stay at your house during the funeral. Before they left, they told me how much they appreciated your hospitality and how your kindness made a difficult time less painful for them. We're fortunate to have such generous neighbors.

For Food

I want to thank you for the meals you brought over while Harry was in the hospital and after he passed. If it hadn't been for you, I probably wouldn't have eaten. I'm fortunate to have a neighbor and friend as thoughtful as you.

Please accept my sister's thanks for the fruit basket you sent her after the loss of her husband. She appreciates your kindness and will thank you herself when she is able.

For Donations

On behalf of my father and our family, I want to thank you for your kind expression of sympathy and the donation you made to the American Cancer Society in my mother's name. She would have been pleased.

How thoughtful of you to make a donation to the scholarship fund in my mother's name at Clinton High School. Your gift means a great deal at our time of loss. As a former teacher, our mother would have been happy to know that a deserving young person will benefit from your generosity.

To Hospital Staff

Our family would like to thank the doctors and nurses at County Hospital for their help during our father's last days. Knowing that he was in such capable hands made dealing with his passing easier. Thank you for your care and compassion. Please accept these flowers as a token of our gratitude.

The Dennison family would like to extend a sincere thank you to the staff of the Hospice Ward at Memorial Hospital. The care you gave our mother during her stay was exceptional. Thank you also for keeping us up to date on her condition. We are sending a donation to your ward in the name of our mother, Florence Hardy.

Thanks For ...

From favors to protecting our country, people give us good reason to say thank you every day. If you've ever found yourself wanting to say thanks for any of the following reasons, here's how.

Favors

You're such an angel to look after the kids every time I go to the supermarket. It's hard to shop when you have three little ones pulling everything off the shelves. Give me a shopping list next time, and I'll get what you need, too. Just call it thanks from one neighbor to another.

Greeting Goofs

Don't neglect the people who do everyday favors for you. Those favors add up over time, and a simple thank you lets them know how much they're appreciated.

Thanks for holding my hand the night Benny walked out. I was a basket case, but your hugs got me through it—that and all the margaritas we drank! I read Bil Keane's *Family Circus* last week and it said "A hug is like a boomerang—you get it back right away." So I'm sending this card. Hugs right back to you.

Volunteering

The hospital auxiliary would like to thank all the volunteers who keep our used clothing store, The Other Shop, open. Author and psychiatrist Sherry Anderson put it best when she said, "Volunteers don't get paid, not because they're worthless, but because they're priceless." Every one of you is priceless.

You're such a gift to our church. The way you put together the flea market with such ease and efficiency was amazing. We never made that much money on a fund-raiser before. We can't thank you enough.

Job Interviews

Thank you for taking the time to meet with me this morning. I enjoyed learning about your company and talking with you about the position of sales manager. As we discussed, my previous experience seems to make me an ideal candidate for the job. I look forward to hearing from you.

The Write Way

Sending a thank you after a job interview is not only courteous, it's smart. It gives you the chance to mention your credentials once again and makes you stand out as an applicant.

I want to thank you for my interview this morning. You took time to show me around the restaurant, and I appreciate it. If you hire me, you won't be disappointed. I learn quickly, and I'll be one of your best waiters before you know it. That's a guarantee. I hope I hear from you soon.

Military

I want to thank you for the effort you are making in Iraq. Maya Angelou said, "How important it is for us to recognize and celebrate our heroes and she-roes!" So I'm sending this note—along with a care package— to let you know I care.

Greeting Goofs

Out of sight, out of mind? We hope not. Don't forget the brave men and women who risk their lives every day to protect us—at home and abroad. A simple thank you can mean more than you know.

You may not hear it often, but I want to say thank you. Thank you for doing your best for the people of Iraq and for protecting our country. As a child, you often helped children who couldn't help themselves. Thank you from a neighbor who noticed then and is noticing now. I'm proud of you.

Firefighters and Emergency Workers

I'd like to thank the people of Fire Company 23 for your help the other night when my stove went up in flames from a grease fire. If it hadn't been for your quick response, we would have lost everything. You are my heroes.

Thank you for saving my daughter's life last Friday. You kept her alive until she reached the hospital, and I am eternally grateful. You could make more money doing something else, but Tom Brokaw said, "It's easy to make a buck. It's a lot tougher to make a difference." You, my friend, made a big difference.

Thank You Blessings

When you'd like to take a spiritual approach to your thank you, use the following for your inspiration.

Religious

I thank God for the blessing you've been to me this past month. You held my hand when I was afraid, you made me laugh when I was nervous, and you helped me believe that God wouldn't give me anything I couldn't handle. The reason I handled it all was because God gave me you as a friend. Thank you, friend.

You're a good friend. You were always there for me when I was going through my chemotherapy treatment. It makes me think of what Tracy Chapman said, "I've seen and met angels wearing the disguise of ordinary people living ordinary lives." Thank you for being my angel.

Spiritual

Buddha once said, "Thousands of candles can be lighted from a single candle, and the life of the candle will not be shortened. Happiness never decreases by being shared." In fact, your candle burns even brighter because of all the people you've helped. Let me be the one to say thank you.

"Too often we underestimate the power of a touch, a smile, a kind word, a listening ear, an honest compliment, or the smallest act of caring, all of which have the potential to turn a life around." Those words by Leo Buscaglia remind me of how your caring friendship has turned my life around. Thank you.

Greeting Goofs

Sending a thank you note late is inconsiderate. But it's better than not sending one at all. Begin your note with a short but sincere apology and then move on to expressing your gratitude.

Quotes to Inspire You

I've learned that you shouldn't go through life with a catchers mitt on both hands. You need to be able to throw something back. —*Maya Angelou*

One can pay back the loan of gold, but one dies forever in debt to those who are kind. —*Malayan proverb*

It is not so much our friends' help that helps us, as the confidence of their help. —*Epicurus*

When eating bamboo sprouts, remember the man who planted them. —*Chinese proverb*

I would thank you from the bottom of my heart, but for you my heart has no bottom. —*Unknown*

It isn't the size of the gift that matters, but the size of the heart that gives it. —*Eileen Elias Freeman in* The Angels' Little Instruction Book

We make a living by what we get, but we make a life by what we give. —*Winston Churchill*

No one is more cherished in this world than someone who lightens the burden of another. Thank you. —*Unknown*

Chapter 9

Get Well and Encouragement

Stores always have lots of get well cards on the racks because many of us would rather let a card do the talking than try to figure out what to say to someone who's sick. Sitting down to write an encouraging note to someone who has had setbacks in his or her life might leave you at a loss for words; it happens to a lot of us. If you don't have a clue what to say, the notes in this chapter help you express yourself sincerely.

Get Well Wishes

People with illnesses need our notes of support and encouragement. But too often, we end up with pens poised, not knowing how to express our feelings. We consulted the card doctor, and she recommended a prescription for the following notes.

For an Illness

I just heard you were diagnosed with diabetes. Ten years ago, my father got the same diagnosis, but thankfully, he followed his doctor's orders about taking care of himself, and today he's doing very well. I'm sending good thoughts your way and hoping you feel better soon.

Greeting Goofs

Never say "I know how you feel." You really don't. Offering support by saying you know what the tests, surgery, or recovery period are like is okay, but only if you've been through the same ordeal.

Your back went out again? You poor thing. Charlie has back problems, too, so I know what a pain (literally) it can be. Please let me know what I can do to make your life easier until you're up and around again.

For Hospital Stays

I'm so sorry you're in the hospital, but I'm so glad you didn't hesitate to call 911 when you had chest pain. I'm sure you must have been very scared. I've heard your doctor is wonderful and that you're coming home in a few days. Great! We missed you at cards this week!

Hollywood producer Samuel Goldwyn once said, "A hospital is no place to be sick." We're all more comfortable in our own homes, but sometimes the hospital is the best place for us, at least for a while. Before long, you'll be well and home again. In the meantime, I'll call and visit. Get well soon.

Greeting Goofs _____

The worst goof you can make is not writing at all because you're not sure what to say. When people are sick, they appreciate every note they get, no matter what you say.

For Accidents

When I heard about your motorcycle accident my heart just about stopped! Thank goodness you were wearing your helmet and only suffered a concussion. When will you feel well enough for visitors? I'll bring the latest copy of *Cycle World*.

Joanne told me you fell on the ice last week and broke your leg. How awful! Please let me know what I can do to help you. Go for groceries? Do some laundry? Run an errand? Or maybe you'd just like some company? Here's hoping you're out of that cast in time for golf season!

For Surgery

What's this I hear about the doctors making you sit on the side of the bed the day after heart surgery? Ouch! But that obviously means you came through with flying colors. Guess all our prayers and good thoughts worked. When will you be up for visitors?

Nineteenth-century humorist Kin Hubbard said, "A bad cold wouldn't be so annoying if it weren't for the advice of our friends." Obviously, a hysterectomy is a lot more annoying than a cold. My advice? Obey the doctor's orders and get well soon! I miss you.

The Write Way _____

Humor is fine if you know the person well and the illness is relatively minor. You can even use mild humor with serious illnesses if the person's doing well.

Get Well Wishes

It literally hits home when people close to you have health problems. Here are some heartfelt words to convey your caring and support.

To Children

Your mom told me you were having your tonsils out next week. I had mine out, too, when I was your age, and the part I remember best is getting lots of ice cream to eat afterward! What's your favorite flavor? Chocolate-chip cookie dough? Strawberry? I'll bring some over and we can have a "make your own sundae" party.

Daniel said you were in the hospital and your class made you a big card that everyone signed. I'm sure my card is not nearly as large as your class card, but I'm also sending along a teddy bear to keep you company and cheer you up. Get well soon, honey!

> **The Write Way**
>
> If the illness isn't serious, focus on how the person will feel better soon and the things you'll do together when he or she recovers.

To Families

When Dad and I found out we had high cholesterol, I taped this quote from humorist Doug Larson on the fridge: "Life expectancy would grow by leaps and bounds if green vegetables smelled as good as bacon." This low-fat cookbook was a life-saver for us, in every sense of the word. *Bon appétit!*

I wish I could be there to wait on you hand and foot. I could make you tea, prop your leg up on pillows, buy you trashy novels and boxes of bonbons, and rent you chick flicks. This card, lots of well wishes, and dozens of "get well soon" phone calls from me will (hopefully) be the next best thing.

To Friends and Neighbors

I was shocked to hear that Jerry had a minor stroke and is in the hospital. You must be so worried. I know how overwhelming hospitalization can be, so please, tell me how I can help. Do you need a ride to the hospital? An errand run? A hand to hold? I'm at your service—now and after Jerry comes home.

When I heard about your disc surgery, I thought, *Poor Michael! Knowing him, he's probably more worried about Tina than himself.* Don't worry. The neighbors are taking turns driving her to the hospital, and she has enough frozen casseroles to last six months! Now just relax and get well.

To Co-Workers

Oh, no! What a terrible way to end a vacation in Vermont—with a skiing accident. Rumor has it that you veered off the beginner slope onto a double diamond—and it was all downhill from there. A broken ankle is no fun, but thank goodness you weren't hurt worse. We miss you here at work, so get well soon!

I'm sorry to hear you have mono. Don't they call that the "kissing disease"? Well, I hope you at least had fun catching it! Seriously, I understand you're feeling pretty tired and that you'll be out of work for a month. I hope you get lots of rest and come back to work good as new.

The Write Way

Tell the sick person how much he's valued by mentioning some activity—like work or the gym—where his presence is missed.

To Church Family

At church today, Pastor Bob announced you were back in the hospital. We prayed they'd find an antibiotic to treat your infection and that you'd be home and back to church soon. The choir just doesn't sound the same without your lovely soprano voice. Get well soon and God bless.

✉ Greeting Goofs

Don't trivialize a person's illness or pain by penning platitudes like "everything will be fine" or "you'll be on your feet soon." Putting more thought and sincerity into your words will make a difference.

At the church coffee hour, people were saying you swerved to miss a deer and lost control of your car. I was so relieved to learn you weren't hurt badly and didn't have to stay overnight in the hospital. I guess next time we see you, you'll be on crutches. Hope you're feeling better soon.

Get Well Blessings

Faith can do wonders toward healing a sick body, and a quick prayer or word of inspiration may be just what someone needs to feel better.

Religious

I'm so sorry to hear you broke your arm! When it gets too much for you, think about Mother Teresa. She said, "I know God will not give me anything I can't handle. I just wish that He didn't trust me so much." Sounds like God trusts you a lot, too! Hope you heal soon.

In Jeremiah 30:17, the Lord says, "I will restore you to health and heal your wounds." Let's ask the Lord to answer our prayer and do the same for you. He alone has the power of healing.

Spiritual

An Arabic proverb says, "He who has health has hope, and he who has hope has everything." You've always had such a zest for life. Don't let this spell of bad health spoil it. Here's to health and hope and everything!

Your mother tells me you've been in a lot of pain since your surgery. What you're going through can't be easy, but maybe this quote from Helen Keller will give you hope: "Although the world is full of suffering, it is full also of the overcoming of it." I hope to see you back to your old self soon.

A Word of Cheer

When life gives you lemons, not everyone feels up to making lemonade. Some events, like getting passed over for a promotion or suffering a major depression, can leave a person feeling like his or her life is in total turmoil. Sending the right note can help people get through these bad times.

For Disappointments and Difficulties

When I heard you didn't get promoted, I was floored. You work so hard, I felt sure you'd get the job. Don't let this crush you. I know you'll consider your alternatives carefully and make the right decision. You're strong and capable, and you have a good head on your shoulders. No wonder I love working with you!

The Write Way

Write a letter of support and encouragement as soon as you hear about someone's setback or disappointment. Keep a positive tone, and avoid any hint of criticism.

Thank you for finally sharing what was bothering you. I'm not surprised you maxed out your credit cards, as you've had a lot of medical expenses lately. I have a number for a credit counseling service, and with some creative budgeting, you'll be back on track in no time. I know you can do it.

For Stress and Depression

Author and speaker Peter Sinclair said, "Depression loses its power when fresh vision pierces the darkness." I know this is a dark time for you, but if you feel like talking, I'm a good listener. And who knows—maybe we'll stumble on that "fresh vision" together.

They say a little stress is healthy, but not the amount you have. It hurts me to see you turning into a nail-biting workaholic. If you can't decrease your hours, maybe it's time to look for a less-demanding job where they appreciate your talents more. There are openings at my company, and I would be more than happy to ask around. Just say the word.

For Caregiving

Now that your dad has moved in, you're probably going through a period of adjustment. If you need advice on juggling work, family, and adult caregiving, there's a great support group at Community Hospital, where I work. Call me if you would like more info or just want to chat.

Taking care of Kelly must be a challenge. Now that she's getting bigger, lifting her in and out of the wheelchair has to be hard on your back. My friend just became a massage therapist, and she'd love some practice. I could watch Kelly while my friend works on your back. How about Thursday afternoon? Are we on?

The Write Way

Offer help to someone if you're available and they really need it. Be specific about what you can do, such as pick up a few groceries, babysit, or provide useful information.

For Weight Loss Programs

You took my advice and joined LA Weight Loss! I'm so glad. It's the only program that's ever worked for me, so I'm telling all my friends about it. I know I sound like a walking advertisement, but who cares? I can't wait to hear how you're doing. Keep me posted on your progress!

You're going to love Weight Watchers. It's such a great program. They teach you strategies at the meetings and offer plenty of recipes and ideas for meal plans online. Best of all, we can be a support for each other! Wait until you see the difference it makes!

For Rehab Treatment

I'm so proud of you for checking into the rehab center. It takes courage to admit you have a problem and even more courage to seek help. You aren't just helping yourself; you're setting an example for your friends who may have drug problems, too. Stay strong, stay focused, and God bless you.

I'm very impressed that you went to your first AA meeting. The first step—and probably the hardest—is owning up to the problem. Your journey will probably have its ups and downs, but I'm rooting for you to succeed. Keep up the good work.

A Word of Cheer

From children to co-workers, everyone can use a boost now and then. These notes of cheer can help someone who's feeling blue start looking for rainbows again.

To Children

Your dad told me you weren't picked for the elementary school orchestra. I know you're disappointed, but don't give up. You play the violin very well, and you've learned a lot in one year. If you keep practicing, you'll be twice as good in two years! I bet they'll beg you to join then. Keep that bow moving!

The Write Way

Kids and teens get down in the dumps, too. It's not always easy to talk to them face to face. Often, you can say in a short note what you can't say in person.

Mommy told me you had a bad day today. You know what? Some days are good and some days are bad. It happens to everyone, even me. Cheer up. I bet tomorrow will be good—for you and for me.

To Family

I wish you'd relax a little, Sis. Since the baby came, it's as if you're competing for the "mother of the year" award. You're a great mom, but you'll turn into a zombie if you don't get some sleep. Here's some free advice from someone who loves you: hire a babysitter and take a nap. The baby will survive. I promise!

I know you had your heart set on running the marathon, Dad, and it's too bad your bum knee acted up. Maybe you can still be involved. I hear they need people on the water brigade, and I'd be happy to go along and help. Whether it's cheering you on or helping you pass out water to the other runners, I'm proud to be with my dad.

To Friends and Neighbors

I hear you've been looking for a job since you and Craig split up. Don't get discouraged. Plenty of positions are out there for a woman with your skills. It's all about marketing. And I know just the right employment agency to call. If you want, I can give you their number. You'll be handing out brand-new business cards in no time!

I'm so sorry you didn't get accepted to Princeton. I know you were hoping to go to an Ivy League school, but there's so much competition, I'll bet you weren't the only valedictorian they passed on. Meanwhile, four other fantastic schools want you, lucky girl! How does it feel to be so popular?

To Co-Workers

I heard that the deal fell through. I know it's discouraging, but worse things could happen. We could run out of coffee and donuts in the lunchroom! Seriously though, you're an excellent businessman, and something good is bound to happen soon. Just be patient. In the meantime, how about some more coffee and donuts?

I know you're disappointed that your book hasn't been published yet, but don't let it get you down. Take Oprah's advice: "Think like a queen. A queen is not afraid to fail. Failure is another stepping-stone to greatness." You're an excellent writer who's destined for greatness. I'll bet my library card on it!

The Write Way

When someone's feeling down, encourage her—tactfully—to try something new. Let her know how much you admire her talents and appreciate what she has to offer.

To Church Family

We've missed you at church lately. I know you've been down since your daughter moved out, and no one likes to be alone. Do you think a new project might interest you? We could use you at our flea market. If you could give us half a day on Saturday, we'd love to see your smiling face again.

I know you're discouraged that you've put on a few pounds and your doctor wants you to take blood pressure medication. You weren't expecting it, but unfortunately, it happens to a lot of us sooner or later. Isn't it great we have the resources to keep us healthy for longer these days? Know that you're not alone in your struggle.

Encouragement Blessings

Inspirational words are a wonderful way to help someone who's depressed or anxious turn things around. See if any of the following words can help you lift up someone who's down.

Religious

The Bible says, "Cast your cares upon the Lord, for he cares about you." (1 Peter 5:7) We care about you, too. May your faith in God help you through this difficult time.

When the apostle Paul worried that he was too weak to do the work of the Lord, God said, "My grace is sufficient for thee: for my strength is made perfect in weakness." (2 Corinthians 12:9) If God could help Paul in his weakness, I'm sure he can also help you. You only need to ask.

Spiritual

I came across this quote by an unknown writer: "I can't change the direction of the wind. But I can adjust my sails." My friend, the past can't be helped, but the future can. Sail into it with hope and vigor.

When you're feeling down and out, here's what Buddha said: "Let us rise up and be thankful, for if we didn't learn a lot today, at least we learned a little, and if we didn't learn a little, at least we didn't get sick, and if we got sick, at least we didn't die; so, let us all be thankful." I am thankful for you.

Quotes to Inspire You

Get well quotes:

The healthy and strong individual is the one who asks for help when he needs it. Whether he's got an abscess on his knee or in his soul. —*Rona Barrett*

The most important thing in illness is never to lose heart. —*Nikolai Lenin*

A good laugh and a long sleep are the best cures in the doctor's book. —*Irish proverb*

Humor is healing. —*Brad Garrett*

Hugs are the universal medicine. —*Unknown*

Encouragement quotes:

Courage doesn't always roar. Sometimes courage is the little voice at the end of the day that says "I will try again tomorrow." —*Artist and writer Mary Anne Radmacher*

It just wouldn't be a picnic without the ants. —*Unknown*

A problem is a chance for you to do your best. —*Duke Ellington*

The greatest glory in living lies not in never failing, but in rising every time we fail. —*Nelson Mandela*

Be of good cheer. Do not think of today's failures, but of the success that may come tomorrow. —*Helen Keller*

Chapter 10

Sympathy and Condolence

Suffering and death. They are two of the most painful subjects to talk about. Writing a sympathy note to someone who is facing a serious illness or has lost a loved one may seem impossible to you, but it's not as difficult as whatever that someone—your friend, your family member, your co-worker—is experiencing. It's moments like these when people really need your love and support.

When Someone Is Seriously Ill

It's not easy to watch someone you love suffer, whether or not there's hope for recovery. A hand-written sympathy note, like one of the following, can help him or her feel less alone.

Cancer

I was so sorry to hear about your diagnosis. I know the next few months are going to be difficult, and my thoughts will be with you as you go through your treatment. It's amazing what doctors and hospitals can accomplish these days. I'm hoping you'll feel better soon.

The Write Way

Without being too specific, write about what's happening to the other person. Offer your sympathy and let him know how much you care about him. Try to be upbeat and optimistic.

I just learned about your cancer, and I want you to know that I am here for you. Belgian writer Henri Nouwen said, "The friend who can be silent with us in a moment of despair or confusion ... who can tolerate not knowing, not curing, not healing ... that is a friend who cares." That's the kind of friend I want to be.

AIDS

I understand you're not feeling well lately. Please know that whatever you are going through, you have friends who care deeply about you. We're hoping you get back on your feet from this latest setback soon.

You've shown so much courage in battling your disease. Despite the ups and downs, you keep coming back strong. We care about you very much, and we trust that you'll pull through this time, too.

Chronic Illnesses

I'm sorry to hear you're having trouble controlling your diabetes. It must be difficult to achieve the correct balance of food and medication, but you've been doing your best to make it work. We're hoping your health improves soon.

Your wife explained that a relapse from multiple sclerosis was keeping you out of work this week. Please don't worry about the office. We'll take care of your clients and any emergencies until you're well enough to return. We're all hoping you feel better soon.

Terminal Illnesses

I'm sorry to hear you're feeling so poorly. I know this is a difficult time for you, and I think about you often. How would you feel about a short visit next weekend? I'll call on Friday to see if you're up to it. Please know how much I love you and care for you.

You've been fighting so hard to battle your illness, you must be exhausted. Try to get some rest for a while. Know that we miss you at our garden club meetings, and we'd be happy to come over and plant some spring bulbs if you don't feel up to it. There's nothing like yellow daffodils to cheer you up. Take care of yourself.

> **Greeting Goofs** _____
>
> Don't send a "get well" card to someone if she's obviously not going to get well. Instead, write your note on a blank card or one that simply says "thinking of you."

Risky Surgeries

Bradley told me you were having a triple bypass next week. You will be in my thoughts and prayers. I hope the surgery is a huge success and you're back to your old self in no time. Don't worry about the plants. I'll take care of them until you're home again.

We were floored when you told us you had a benign brain tumor. But you've been so calm and optimistic, it's helped all of us feel that way, too. You have a wonderful outlook, Aleta, and that will only help in your recovery after surgery. God bless you.

People in Hospice Care

We hear your health hasn't been good lately, and we wanted to let you know how much we care and how very much your friendship means to us. Someone once said, "A hug is the shortest distance between friends." We can't be with you, dear friend, but we're sending you our hugs to let you know how close you are in our hearts.

I'm sorry you're so tired all the time. I can't take away your fatigue, but I can give you some company if you feel up to it. I might even bring along a deck of cards—in case you're in the mood to lose a little money. What'll it be, poker or rummy?

Greeting Goofs

Don't mention death when writing to people who are terminally ill—unless they bring it up first. Some people will want to talk about it, while others won't.

Military-Related Injuries

Your mom told us you're in a VA hospital because of an injury you received in Iraq. We were saddened to hear you lost your leg, but we pray that your strong and determined spirit will get you back on the road to recovery soon. We're grateful for the sacrifices you've made and pray for you every day.

> ### The Write Way _____
>
> If you know any wounded soldiers, write to them, especially if they've been hospitalized. Hospitals can be lonely places, and a note of support and appreciation can make someone smile.

We're so grateful you survived the injuries you sustained in Afghanistan. Hospital life can be frustrating, but we hope that with patience and the medical technology available you'll make a full recovery. Our touch football games haven't been the same without you. We're hoping you're back to play with us soon.

Families and Friends of Patients

It's tough when your best friend is sick, and I know you miss seeing him every day. The best we can do is hope that the surgery and radiation will work and he'll recover. Keep being a good friend and a good listener. He needs you now more than ever. So do we.

Maryanne told me the sad news about her father, your husband, being diagnosed with lung cancer. Although I can't begin to understand what you're feeling, please know you and your family are in my thoughts and prayers.

The Write Way

Don't forget the patient's family and friends. A serious illness can have a profound impact on them. Write a short note to let them know you care.

Sympathy Blessings

With few exceptions, people who are seriously ill don't mind people praying for them, even when they're not religious. That doesn't mean you should start quoting from the Bible for everyone, but some people will appreciate it.

Religious

As you go through this latest round of treatments, my only wish for you is that "The Lord bless you and keep you; the Lord make his face shine upon you and be gracious to you; the Lord turn his face toward you and give you peace." (Numbers 6:24–26) My thoughts and prayers are with you.

It's difficult to face illness alone; that's why it helps to have friends for support. But no one can give you more strength than God. Remember Psalm 46:1—"God is our refuge and strength, an ever-present help in trouble." May he give you the strength you need to get through this time of trouble.

Spiritual

The dignity with which you handle your illness never ceases to amaze us. Inspirational writer Stephen Covey said, "To touch the soul of another human being is to walk on holy ground." You have touched our souls with your courage and strength. We pray every day for your healing.

Buddha said, "Our sorrows and wounds are healed only when we touch them with compassion." May the people who surround you heal your wounds with love and compassion. And may you do the same for yourself. We love you.

The Loss of a Loved One

Grief is a private matter, and people experience it in different ways. But there's one thing everyone has in common: the need for love and support. Writing a personal note is a good way to show you care.

Infants and Young Children

Words can't express how I feel about Tina's death. How can such a happy occasion become such a sad one? I don't pretend to have any answers; just know that I care and I'm here for you.

The Write Way

The loss of an infant or a young child is especially devastating. It's a poor time for advice or platitudes. Just be honest and sincere in your writing, and let the couple know you feel for them.

You worked so tirelessly to find treatment for Alex. Your son's life was a treasure, even as brief as it was, and we'll never forget him. We love you and we share your grief.

Teen and Adult Sons and Daughters

We were so sorry to hear about Grady's death. He was a fine young man and we'll remember him fondly. It's always so difficult when a young person dies. We can only hope that in time, memories of your dear son will bring you comfort.

You daughter Lisa was a beautiful woman, and it's so very sad that she's gone. I'm going to miss her smile and her laughter. She lit up any room she entered. I'm lucky I could call her my friend. You—and the world—have lost a special person.

Spouses

We just heard the news about Lew's death. We would have attended his funeral but were away at the time. Please accept our deepest sympathy. He was a good friend and a true gentleman. If there's anything we can do—help with the children or lend a comforting shoulder to lean on—we're here for you.

✉ Greeting Goofs

Be tactful with someone who's lost a spouse. Avoid remarks like "you'll find someone to marry again." And don't add to a young child's stress with comments like "you're the man of the family now."

Words can't adequately express how sorry I am about Gina's death. She was a devoted wife, a loving mother, and a true friend. She was also the funniest person I've ever met, the life of every party. She'll live in my memory, and in my heart, forever.

Life Partners

I was heartsick to learn about Dorothy's passing. Not many couples are as close as you were. I hope that your memories of Dorothy will get you through this difficult time. I cared about both of you and my heart aches for your loss.

✏ The Write Way

Always mention the name of the deceased person—if you know it. Your note will sound more personal.

What a tragedy Adam's death was. Someone with that much talent should live to be 100—that's how much he had to contribute to the world. He loved life, he loved his friends, and he loved you. All our lives are richer for having known him. My heart goes out to you.

Parents

We were saddened to hear about Leona's death. Your mother was an amazing person, and I loved her dearly. She wrote wonderful poetry, played the piano beautifully, and made friends with everyone in our neighborhood. You've suffered a great loss—as have we. Our thoughts and prayers are with your family.

It made me sad to hear that your father died. He was a wonderful person, and I know you'll miss him very much. Sometimes life doesn't seem fair, does it? I lost my father when I was 10 years old, too. If you ever want someone to talk to, I'm here for you.

Stepparents

I was sorry to hear about your stepmother's death. Barbara was a friend, even before she married your father. I knew you two became close over time. Please accept my condolences on your loss. She was a remarkable woman.

Bruce and I are so sorry to hear about the death of your stepfather, Ben. The last time we talked, you said he and your mother were taking a cross-country trip in their motor home. Sounds like they had some great times together. My thoughts are with you. I know you'll miss him.

Grandparents

I can't believe your grandmother's gone. At 85, Millie was an amazing woman. The neighborhood thought of her as their unofficial grandmother, too, and she was always ready to help everyone. Our hearts go out to you. We have all lost someone very special.

What can I say about your grandmother, Rose? She loved playing poker, read three books a week, did crossword puzzles with a pen, and went to the gym until she was 90. In other words, she lived every day to the hilt! Here's to her life and the example she set for all of us. We'll miss her.

The Write Way _____

Celebrate the life of the person instead of focusing on his death. Write a personal anecdote or describe the qualities you admired in him.

Other Family

We were sorry to hear about your uncle's death. Everyone at the senior center loved Herb. He enjoyed playing cards and helping out with the yard sales. He may have passed away, but his memory still lives with us. Please accept our condolences.

Please accept our sympathy on the death of your cousin Robert. Although we only spent one weekend with him at your vacation house, we'll always remember his warmth and wit. The kids still talk about how he taught them to catch frogs in the pond. He will be missed.

Friends

I know your friendship with Dennis was very special to you. In fact, you once said you thought of him as a brother. I'm sure you must be hurt by his loss. I want you to know that I care and am thinking of you.

When Ringo Starr sang about getting by with a little help from his friends, I think he was singing about you and Leslie. What a one-person support group she was for you—and you for her! You must be devastated by her death, and I'm so sorry for your loss. Please tell me how I can help.

Pets

To say good-bye to your dog is to lose a little piece of your heart. Wilbur was a good, sweet dog. He was lucky to have great "parents" like you. Any creature who loves us unconditionally must have a special place in heaven, don't you think? An angel is probably rubbing his tummy right now.

A cat can be a good companion. When you lose one, you feel as if your best friend is gone. Sam was more than a cat to you. He was a member of your family. Saying good-bye to him must have broken your heart. We're thinking of you.

The Write Way

Write more than once. Grief is a process that can take years to unfold. Christmas, a birthday, and anniversaries of a death are especially difficult. Your thoughts will be appreciated.

Sudden Losses

Death is difficult in itself, but when it strikes suddenly or with tragic implications, the grief process can be even more of a challenge. These notes are the hardest to write ... but the most needed.

Unexpected Death

I was shocked when I heard the news about Jack's sudden heart attack. He was so young and full of life, it's impossible to comprehend that he's no longer with us. I can't even begin to know how you and Chris must be feeling. My heart goes out to both of you.

Greeting Goofs

Avoid such euphemisms as: "it's all for the best," "I know how you feel," "time heals all things," or "she's in a better place." Just write honestly and sincerely.

We're still reeling from the news of Jim's fatal accident. The four of us had so much in common, I thought we'd be friends and traveling companions forever. We can't believe he's gone, and we can only imagine what you're going though. Please call us, day or night, anytime you need a shoulder. We're here for you.

Military Death

Your daughter Amber died defending her country. I imagine you feel so much pride for her courage as well as so much grief for her loss. My heart goes out to you.

Bud gave the ultimate sacrifice—his life for his country. But even if your child is in the military, you're never prepared to lose him. Please know we're thinking of you and praying for you. Bud was a true hero.

Suicides

Words are so difficult at a time like this. And there are no easy answers. All I can say is that I'm sorry to hear about the death of your son, Andrew. I hope being surrounded by family and friends gives you strength during this unbelievably difficult time. My thoughts are with you.

The Write Way

When someone commits suicide, survivors often feel guilt and confusion. The best way to handle your note is not to focus on *how* the person died. Look deep into your heart, and the words will come.

I wish I had the right words to express how profoundly sad I feel about the sudden loss of your wife. Danielle was a special person who touched the lives of everyone she met. I miss her terribly. My heart aches for you.

Miscarriages and Stillbirths

I'm so sorry to hear about your loss. To almost reach the end of your pregnancy and lose the baby must be a crushing blow. Please accept the sympathy of everyone in the office. Take as much time as you need before you return to work. We care so much about you.

Greeting Goofs

Don't write to a couple about a miscarriage unless one of them has told you about it. When you do write, don't forget it's the husband's loss, too.

David told me about your miscarriage. I'm so sorry. I know how excited you both were about having a second baby. I'm thinking of you at this sad time and hoping you'll feel better soon.

Condolence Blessings

What better time to send a religious or inspirational note than after the loss of a loved one? Just a reminder: not everyone is a believer. Be sure the person who's receiving the note will be comfortable with what you say.

Religious

What a great guy your dad was. I really miss him. It makes me think of a verse from Matthew, chapter 5: "Blessed are they that mourn, for they shall be comforted." We can comfort each other, but our greatest comfort is in knowing that Howard is with God. May he rest in peace forever.

Mother Teresa once said, "Death is nothing else but going home to God, the bond of love will be unbroken for all eternity." You must miss your sister terribly, but I hope you can find some comfort in knowing that Diane has gone home again.

Spiritual

I'm sorry about the death of your wife, Shirley. When I miss someone I love, I look up at the stars and think of this Eskimo legend: "Perhaps, they are not stars in the sky, but rather openings where our loved ones shine down to let us know they are happy."

We all miss Anna terribly. There's a Buddhist saying I came across once that I hope might help: "When you are born, you cry, and the world rejoices. When you die, you rejoice, and the world cries." While we walk around with tears in our eyes, it's a comfort to know that Anna is somewhere rejoicing.

Quotes to Inspire You

Sympathy quotes:

When the heart weeps for what it has lost, the spirit laughs for what it has found. —*Sufi proverb*

Earth has no sorrow that Heaven cannot heal. —*Unknown*

The greatest healing therapy is friendship and love. —*Hubert H. Humphrey*

Courage is being afraid but going on anyhow. —*Dan Rather*

Eventually you will come to understand that love heals everything, and love is all there is. —*Gary Zukav*

Condolence quotes:

When you are sorrowful look again in your heart, and you shall see that in truth you are weeping for that which has been your delight. —*Kahlil Gibran*

It is foolish and wrong to mourn the men who died. Rather we should thank God that such men lived. —*George S. Patton Jr.*

To live in hearts we leave behind is not to die. —*Thomas Campbell*

Grief can't be shared. Everyone carries it alone, his own burden, his own way. —*Anne Morrow Lindbergh*

For everything there is a season, and a time for every matter under heaven: A time to be born, and a time to die ... —*Ecclesiastes 3:1–2*

Chapter 11

Other Losses

How often do you "lose" something small—your keys or maybe a thought? It happens all the time, right? But what if you lose your house or your job? Or a relationship? Or the ability to live independently? The loss could turn your life upside down. When it happens to people you care about, they need to know you're there for them.

Breaking Up

As the song goes, "breaking up is hard to do"—and not just for the couple. It also has a ripple effect on the people around them. You can't mend a broken heart, but you can share an encouraging note to let others know you're thinking of them.

Announcing the Breakup

Bill and I have decided to separate for a while. I realize it may come as a surprise, but we needed some space to resolve our problems. I'll be staying with my friend Janine at 35 Grove Street, Arlington, MA 02474. I hope we can count on your support.

It's over. I've asked Eric for a divorce, and he's agreed. He's now living at 529 Shore Drive. I don't want to go into details about it; all you need to know is that I've been hurting for a long time and it's time to move on. I hope you can support me in this decision because I really need it.

The Write Way

When announcing a breakup, handwrite it. Include any necessary contact information, a personal statement (if you want), and your hopes for future communication.

I regret to say that Michelle and I won't be getting married next month as planned. We've decided to break our engagement. Thank you for your love and support.

Separations

I understand that you and Bill have decided to take some time off from each other. Stepping back might be just what you need and will give you time to sort out your problems. Maybe you'll find a way to make it work, but if you can't, I hope both of you find happiness.

Greeting Goofs

The last thing a separated or divorcing couple needs is your judgment. Don't make suggestions or advise them to stay together "for the sake of the kids." Just offer your support.

I just read your note about the separation. I'm sorry to hear that you and Pam are having such serious marriage difficulties. Of course, you have my support. So does Pam. I love you both and hope you can resolve your problems in a way that works best for both of you.

Divorces

Richard and I are saddened that you and Lisa are getting a divorce. It will be difficult, I'm sure, for Zach and Emmy. If there's anything we can do as grandparents, don't hesitate to ask. We think about you and hope that you'll both find a brighter future. We love you both very much.

Your note just arrived. It's not the divorce that upsets Dad and me, it's that you've been hurting for so long. We felt there was a problem between you and Eric, but we didn't want to pry. Of course, we support you. We love you. And when—or if—you feel like talking about it, we're ready to listen.

Life Partner Breakups

We are deeply sorry that you and Joe are breaking up. You are both so dear to us. All we want is for the two of you to be happy. We'd hoped that meant being together, but we love you both even apart.

 Greeting Goofs _____

> Don't take sides in a breakup, no matter how you feel, and don't ask for details. Simply offer your support and your hope for a better future.

I felt your pain when you told me Carol walked out on you. I know you didn't want to give up. Someone once said, "Giving up doesn't always mean you are weak; sometimes it means that you are strong enough to let go." I wish you strength in dealing with what's happened and hope for happier times for you.

 **The Write Way** _____

> It's often easier to say in a note something you can't say in person. Get your thoughts together and write a couple drafts until you're satisfied your note is clear and tactful.

Engagement Breakups

I'm so sorry to hear you and Michelle split up and are calling off the wedding. You two loved each other, and what happened is your business. As your friend, let me know if there's anything I can do to help you through this time.

The Write Way

Keep your note short. Mention the breakup, extend your sympathy, offer specific help if you can, and finish with hope for a better future.

Leslie told me you've cancelled the wedding. I'm sorry it didn't work out with you and Josh. I read this quote: "Relationships are like glass. Sometimes it's better to leave them broken than try to hurt yourself putting them back together." You deserve the best—and I'm sure it's out there for you.

Breaking Up a Business

Even business partners have breakups—for financial or personal reasons. Here's how to announce a breakup and offer support for someone who's going through one.

Announcing the Breakup

I never thought I'd have to say this, but Jeff and I are ending our partnership in the business. He'll be working as a wedding consultant for Dream Weddings in New York. My new shop, Mark's Floral Creations, will still design quality floral arrangements as before. I hope to continue doing business with you.

It's my sad duty to inform you that Ted Branson has decided to end our partnership to become Sipco's financial manager. We've added two accountants to our team, and I assure you that our new firm, Cobb and Associates, will continue to provide excellent services to our clients. We look forward to maintaining our business with you.

Business Partner Breakups

I'm so sorry you and Jeff have ended your partnership in Jeff and Mark's Floral Creations. You were a terrific team. I wish Jeff success in his new job as a wedding consultant for Dream Weddings, and I'm confident that Mark's Floral Creations will be as exciting and creative as ever. Glad to do business with you.

It's a sad day when a long and successful partnership comes to an end. I wish Ted Branson the best as new financial manager of Sipco. Meanwhile, Cobb and Associates can be assured of our continued business and support.

Breakup Blessings

A religious or inspirational card for a breakup? Why not? Love is a universal condition. In fact, it's the basis of countless religions. If you think it's appropriate, here are a few ideas.

Religious

I know your heart was broken when George left. I hope you'll find comfort in this old Jewish saying: "God is closest to those with broken hearts." Let him heal you.

You went into your marriage with such love and confidence 10 years ago. Now it's over and your heart is broken. Someone once said, "God can heal a broken heart, but he has to have all the pieces." Why not give God the pieces so he can put your heart together again?

Spiritual

The trouble with breakups is that sometimes you miss the other person. Kahlil Gibran said, "Ever has it been that love knows not its own depth until the hour of separation." Think of it as the memory of a love that's gone. A new love is waiting for you, but you have to let go of the past so you can embrace it.

Ever since the divorce, you've tried so hard to pick up the pieces and move on. I'm worried you haven't allowed yourself to say good-bye to the love that once existed between the two of you. "Let your tears come," said Eileen Mayhew. "Let them water your soul." Only then will you really be able to move on.

Dealing With Loss

Elie Wiesel said, "Just as despair can come to one only from other human beings, hope, too, can be given to one only by other human beings." When someone you know is despondent because of a loss, who better to give him hope than you? Here's how to do it.

Losing Your Independence

I know you're upset about giving up your apartment and moving in with us. After being your own boss, it must be hard to depend on us for a change. We still admire you, Dad, and we look forward to giving you what you've given us all your life—your love and support. If we work as a team, we can make it happen.

⬜ **Greeting Goofs** _____

Don't take the elderly for granted. Imagine how you'd feel in their situation—because someday you might well be! If someone you know is losing his independence, be considerate of his feelings.

I'm sorry you have to leave for assisted living. We'll miss you at bingo. We all like to have things our own way, but the older we get, the harder it seems to be to manage. Just remember it's your leg that's broken, not your brain. Be nice to the people who help you, and they'll be nice in return. That's my motto. See you soon.

Losing Your Job

I can't believe you lost your job. You poured your heart into that business for 15 years. It won't be easy for them to manage without you, but that's not your problem. Now another company will get to work with the best manager in the business—you. It's just a matter of time.

The Write Way

When writing to someone who's lost a job, be optimistic. Lost work means lost money, probably for several months. Express confidence in the person's ability to find a new job soon.

It's discouraging when a person as capable as you loses her job. Maybe it's time for a change. Roman emperor Marcus Aurelius said, "Loss is nothing else but change, and change is Nature's delight." Why not take this opportunity to find a new kind of work—something that will "delight" you? That'll show 'em!

Losing Your Home

I'm so sorry to hear you've lost your home. I read once that "real loss only occurs when you lose something that you love more than yourself." Losing a home is bad, but you still have your family and friends, and we can help you through this time. We're all in your corner.

I heard the bad news—the bank is threatening to foreclose on your home. You must be crazy with worry. I enclosed an article about a couple who went to a debt management company that worked with the mortgage lenders to create a payback plan. It might work for you, too. Be strong and believe in yourself. You can do it.

> **The Write Way** _____
>
> The loss of a home can be devastating. Sympathize with the person, offer help if you can, and end your note with a vote of confidence that the future will be positive.

Losing Your Business

I'm so sorry you lost your landscaping business. It was a great idea, and your work is brilliant. It just didn't have time to get off the ground. Take heart. Next time business will be better. You might have to work with another company for a while, but you'll be back—bigger and better than ever.

Oh no! I'm devastated that Tout Sweet is going out of business. Every morning, I stop on my way to work for coffee and a biscotti. No one deserved success more than you, but the bakery business can be hard, especially in this economy. Good luck in your future endeavors from one of your many loyal customers.

Bankruptcies

I know it was difficult for you to file for bankruptcy. You've always believed in paying your way, but sometimes life deals you so many bad hands, it can feel overwhelming. I'm sure you'll be back in the game again soon. You have a lot of friends who are rooting for you.

Most people don't know what to say when a friend files for bankruptcy, so they avoid saying anything. This must be very, very hard for you, but please don't turn away from your friends, even the ones who don't know what to say. We're here for you, and we want to help.

Sudden Losses

We're seldom prepared for disaster to strike us, whether it's natural (a flood or a fire) or man-made (someone stealing your car or your wallet). If a person you know suffers a sudden loss, send a few words of sympathy. These notes show you how.

Victims of Crime

I was stunned to hear you were robbed in the parking lot of the mall last week. How frightening. I'm sorry you lost your wallet and credit cards, but I'm grateful you weren't hurt. If you're nursing any emotional scars because of it, I know someone who can help. Please take care of yourself.

What a dreadful way to end a vacation—coming home to find your house has been robbed. It's a good thing you had a list of your possessions to show the insurance company. Of course, it's the sentimental objects we really miss and no one can replace them. I don't know what to say except I'm sorry it happened to you.

Victims of Natural Disaster

I heard you lost your home in the tornado that ripped through your county last week. I can't imagine how you must feel. Saying you were lucky to get out alive isn't much of a consolation. If there's anything we can do—clothes, money, a place to stay—please let us know. We want to be there for you until you get back on your feet—no matter how long it takes.

We saw your house on fire last night. Thank goodness you were able to get everyone out, because smoke inhalation can be life-threatening. The neighborhood is collecting money and clothes to help until you get your insurance payment. Please accept them. We know you'd have done the same for any one of us. We're all just relieved you're okay.

> **The Write Way** _____
>
> Natural disaster victims often suffer more than one loss—from their homes to the lives of family members. They need help but might be too proud to ask. Offer sympathy and assistance, but do it tactfully. Above all, let them know you care.

Blessings for Other Losses

When someone suffers a loss, you can turn to God and the mysteries of existence—both in real life and in your note. One of the following notes might be just what you're looking for.

Religious

I'm sure you cried plenty of tears as you sifted through the charred remains of what was once your home. Tears are what life is about sometimes. But it's also about something else, as verse 5 from Psalm 126 reminds us: "They that sow in tears shall reap in joy." I look forward to sharing joy with you again someday.

Since you lost your job, you've probably lost sleep, worrying about how to start all over again. I don't have the answer, but writer Mary C. Crowley does. She said, "Every evening I turn my worries over to God. He's going to be up all night anyway." I'm sure it would work for you, too. Sleep well, friend.

Spiritual

I wonder, sometimes, why you were assaulted. You're a good person and you didn't deserve it. Indian spiritual leader Sathya Sai Baba said, "Gain and loss, birth and death are in the hands of God." I guess there are some things in life we can't control—or understand. All we can do is accept them and move on.

I know you're frustrated about failing college. This quote from Buddha may help: "Through zeal, knowledge is gotten; through lack of zeal, knowledge is lost; let a man who knows the double path of gain and loss thus place himself that knowledge may grow." You know the double path now; choose well.

Quotes to Inspire You

Quotes about breaking up:

Maybe part of loving is learning to let go. —The Wonder Years

The loss of love is not nearly as painful as our resistance to accepting it is. —*Internet breakup guru Tigress Luv*

I refuse to let what happened to me make me bitter. I still completely believe in love, and I'm open to anything that will happen to me. —*Nicole Kidman*

No matter who broke your heart, or how long it takes to heal, you'll never get through it without your friends. —*Carrie from* Sex and the City

Families break up when people take hints you don't intend and miss hints you do intend. —*Robert Frost*

Quotes about losses:

The soul would have no rainbow if the eyes had no tears. —*Native American Minquass proverb*

We must accept finite disappointment, but never lose infinite hope. —*Martin Luther King Jr.*

The Lord God will wipe all tears from all their faces. —*Isaiah 25:8*

Oh, my friend, it's not what they take away from you that counts. It's what you do with what you have left. —*Hubert H. Humphrey*

I don't think of all the misery but of the beauty that still remains. —*Anne Frank*, The Diary of a Young Girl

Chapter 12

Apologies and Forgiveness

When Elton John sang, "Sorry seems to be the hardest word," everyone knew what he meant. Apologizing can be difficult, but it only hurts for a minute. *Not* apologizing can stay with you forever. The same goes for accepting or rejecting an apology. The notes in this chapter help you say the right thing—after you've said or done the wrong thing. They also help you accept an apology sincerely.

Making an Apology

Saying "I'm sorry" in writing gives you time to choose your words carefully and is the perfect prelude to a verbal apology. Here's some suggestions on how to set things right.

Children's Misconduct

I'm mortified that Jessica broke the vase at your house yesterday. I always watch her closely because she's so inquisitive, but somehow, she got out of my line of vision. Please accept my apologies and this check. Next week, let's get together at my house where there's nothing left to break!

The Write Way

Follow up your written apology with a verbal one. Otherwise, your note might look like the coward's way out. If the person lives out of town, write and then call them to say "I'm sorry."

Seth and I want to apologize for Aaron's irresponsible behavior. You hired him to mow your lawn, and he didn't keep his part of the bargain. We had a serious talk with him about responsibility, and he plans to apologize to you in person. Don't worry if you've hired another lawn mower. We understand.

Pet's Misconduct

I'm so sorry our dog scared you when you walked past our house yesterday. Woody has always been harmless, but animals are unpredictable. From now on, we'll keep him on a leash or in the house. Thanks for being so understanding and for telling us that he was barking at passersby.

How embarrassing. We had no idea Snookums was going over to your yard to do her business. Although that's common behavior for dogs, you're not a pet owner so we don't blame you for being upset. We promise to keep her on a leash from now on. Please let us know how much the shoes cost so we can replace them.

Property Damage

Please accept my apologies for taking out your mailbox last night. When I rounded the turn, I was stunned by the shear multitude of Christmas decorations on your property. Your mailbox was the only object not illuminated, and I didn't see it. Let me know the replacement cost, and I'll send you a check.

The Write Way _____

When your note is an apology for damaging someone's property, always offer to pay restitution.

A thousand apologies for damaging the hood of your car the other day. If I'd known my grandson had an arm like that, we'd have gone to the park to practice. I'm just thankful the baseball didn't hit one of you. Please call me as soon as you get the estimate, and I'll contact my insurance company.

Insensitive Remarks

I'm ashamed of myself for the remark I made today about your dress. We always kid each other about having bad taste in clothes, but what I said sounded truly insulting, although I didn't mean it that way. Actually, I liked your dress and admire your eclectic taste. It's a lot like mine. Truce?

Please forgive me for the comments you overheard me make about your girlfriend. Not knowing you were in the room is no excuse. I shouldn't talk about people I don't know. I'm sure she's a lovely person—especially if you care about her. I hope you forgive me and we can get back on a good footing soon.

Inappropriate Behavior

I'm humiliated beyond words. I not only made a fool of myself, but also spilled an entire plate of food on your rug. I feel I owe everyone an apology, but most of all you. I hope I didn't spoil your lovely party. Please forgive me.

 Greeting Goofs

Don't blame your behavior on someone or something else. Take responsibility for your actions and offer a sincere apology.

I feel awful that Chuck and I had a quarrel at your dinner party last night. I didn't mean to stomp out so rudely. It must have been awkward for you, especially in front of your other guests. I'm sorry. Your friendship means everything to me. I hope you're able to forgive me.

Betraying a Secret

Jennifer, I'm so sorry I slipped and told Allison that you're seeing a therapist. Someone once said, "Friendship isn't a big thing—it's a million little things." Betraying your confidence was a big thing. Will you forgive me and let me make it up to you? Friends like you are one in a million.

 The Write Way

How soon should you write a note of apology? Usually, ASAP. On the other hand, if the person is very angry, giving her a few days to cool off before apologizing in writing might be wise.

I can't believe I thoughtlessly told Frank about your credit card balance. I can't take those words back, and I can't keep Frank from being mad at you. But as Henry David Thoreau once said, "The most I can do for my friend is simply be his friend." That is, I can if you'll let me. I'm so sorry.

Apologies Blessings

Religious leaders of all faiths have wise words to say about forgiveness. If you're sure the recipient will appreciate it, use a religious quote or spiritual sentiment to express your apology.

Religious

"Forgive us our trespasses as we forgive those who trespass against us"—The Lord's Prayer. Although I've said these words hundreds of times, they never really hit home until now. I pray that you'll find it in your heart to forgive me for hurting you.

After our fight yesterday, I wanted someone to tell me I was right and you were wrong. Then this quote from Proverbs 26:20 came to mind: "Without wood a fire goes out; without gossip a quarrel dies down." I realized I needed to talk to you and say, "I'm sorry." To be right is not worth losing a friendship.

Spiritual

Mahatma Gandhi said, "The weak can never forgive. Forgiveness is the attribute of the strong." You're the strongest person I know. Please forgive me.

✉ Greeting Goofs _____

Choose your religious quotes or inspirational words carefully, even when apologizing to someone you know is a churchgoer. Otherwise, it's easy to sound manipulative.

The Write Way _____

It's best to send a forgiveness letter only after getting a request for one. That's not to say you can't forgive someone in your heart. Holding a grudge will only make you unhappier.

Theologian and writer Lewis B. Smedes said, "It takes one person to forgive; it takes two people to be reunited." You say I don't need to apologize for hurting you, but I do. Otherwise, we can never be friends again in the same way. For the sake of our friendship, I'm so sorry. Please forgive me.

Accepting an Apology

Eighteenth-century English poet Alexander Pope wrote, "To err is human, to forgive divine." We've all made mistakes or said something we wish we could take back. But it's easy to forget that when we're the injured party. The notes in this section guide you in sincerely accepting an apology.

Children's Misconduct

Of course I forgive Jessica for breaking my vase. I won't lie and say it wasn't precious to me. But Jessica is also precious. She's too young to understand what she's done and there's really no replacing the vase, so I'm returning the check to you. I will, however, take you up on meeting at your house next time.

Thanks for your note about Aaron. We're disappointed he stopped mowing our lawn, but we think he's a good kid and we'd be glad to offer him a second chance when he comes over to apologize. If he really doesn't want the job, can you recommend someone else?

Greeting Goofs _____

Accepting someone's apology doesn't mean you accept their behavior. Never reply to an apology by saying, "It's okay."

Pet's Misconduct

It was nice of you to write and apologize. I'm very relieved that you've decided to keep your dog tied up or in the house. I was afraid I'd have to find a new walking route. As a dog owner myself, I know how territorial dogs can be. If you'll pardon the pun, I'm glad we nipped this problem in the bud.

Thank you for the apology about Snookums. Although I've never owned a dog, I can't blame her for answering nature's call on my lawn. A leash should solve the problem. As for the shoes, they were an old pair I use for gardening. Perhaps Snookums would like to keep them now—for teething purposes, of course.

Property Damage

Thank you for offering to replace the mailbox you ran into with your car. Fortunately, our homeowner's insurance will cover the damage. We're just glad you weren't hurt when you were "stunned" by our Christmas lights. Come over sometime (drive slowly!) and we'll give you a tour through Christmas-land.

I appreciate your apology. Your grandson has grown so big it's probably better for him—and less dangerous for us—that he practice ball at the park. Let's not allow this one incident to come between neighbors. I'm sure our insurance companies can handle the damage to my car's hood without any help from us.

The Write Way

If someone offers a gesture of peace, accept it. If you're not ready to do it, then you're not ready to forgive. Remember the point—to reconcile your relationship.

Insensitive Remarks

I'm still not convinced you liked my dress, although you're right about my taste being eclectic. However, I do believe you're sorry you insulted me, so I'll forgive you. Maybe I was being a little too sensitive, given our history of teasing each other. So I'll agree to a truce if you agree to lunch someday soon.

Greeting Goofs

Don't accept an apology without giving it some thought first. Are you sure the person is sincere? By the same token, are you sure your reply is honest?

I was surprised at your negative remarks about my girlfriend. I always saw you as sensitive to people. My first reaction was I don't know you! I'm willing to change my mind because you changed yours. You're right about my girlfriend. She's a lovely person and I do care about her. I care about you, too.

Inappropriate Behavior

I forgive you. You're not the first person to have too much to drink at a party. I did it myself once and learned two tricks that I'll share with you: (1) never drink on an empty stomach, and (2) nurse a glass of water between drinks. You can try my tricks on Saturday. I'm having a party, and I'd love you to come.

We always enjoy Chuck's and your company, but your argument did make things a bit awkward for my other guests. The next time the situation arises (if there is a next time), you might want to call and cancel. It's better to work out your problems than to try to stifle them in front of others.

Betraying a Secret

At first I was upset that you told Allison about the therapist—especially after I asked you not to. And I can't say I'm happy she knows. But I was always able to trust you in the past, and I can't imagine not having you around to talk with. I think you're one in a million, too, so let's put it behind us and move on.

The Write Way

Be honest about your feelings. If you were hurt, admit it. It takes a real commitment to forgive someone. After you've done it, make up your mind to let go of it.

I was furious you told Frank about my credit card balance. He was angry at first, but the next day we worked out a budget for me to follow. I guess you could say it all turned out for the best. That doesn't mean I'm happy you betrayed my trust, but you've been a good friend and I know you're sorry. I forgive you.

Forgiveness Blessings

Mark Twain said, "Forgiveness is the fragrance that the violet sheds on the heel that has crushed it." Reading inspirational words can put you in the right frame of mind to accept an apology. Or you can use some of the following in your note.

Religious

Reading your letter of apology made me remember what Jesus said: "If your brother sins, rebuke him, and if he repents, forgive him." (Luke 17:3) I realize now that you didn't hurt me deliberately. So let's put the past behind us and move on, friend. I forgive you.

When you wrote that you were sorry for arguing with me, you said our friendship was more important than being right. I wanted to be right, too. But being angry at you didn't make me feel better—just sad. So I accept your apology and I offer my own to you. If God can forgive us everything, who are we to question?

Spiritual

In the words of Buddha, "Holding onto anger is like grasping a hot coal with the intent of throwing it at someone else—you are the one who gets burned." I'm letting my anger go. I accept your apology. Let's move on, okay?

You asked if I would forgive you for hurting me. I'll be honest. At first I wanted to hurt you back. Then I recalled what Mahatma Gandhi said: "If we practice an eye for an eye and a tooth for a tooth, soon the whole world will be blind and toothless." Let's end the hurt before it gets any worse. I forgive you, friend.

Quotes to Inspire You

Quotes about apologies:

In some families, *please* is described as the magic word. In our house, however, it was *sorry. —Margaret Laurence*

An apology is the superglue of life. It can repair just about anything. *—Cartoonist Lynn Johnston*

Never ruin an apology with an excuse. *—Journalist Kimberly Johnson*

Play fair. Don't hit people. Say you're sorry when you hurt somebody. *—Robert Fulghum*

The most important trip you may take in life is meeting people halfway. *—Author and songwriter Henry Boye*

Quotes about forgiveness:

The practice of forgiveness is our most important contribution to the healing of the world. —*Marianne Williamson*

He who forgives ends the argument. —*African proverb*

Good words do not last long unless they amount to something. —*Chief Joseph*

When a deep injury is done us, we never recover until we forgive. —*South African writer Alan Paton*

Without forgiveness, there's no future. —*Desmond Tutu*

Chapter 13

End-of-the-Year Holidays

Who doesn't look forward to December? The last month of the year is jam-packed with great holidays like Christmas, Hanukkah, and Kwanzaa. There's something for everyone—from singing carols to lighting the menorah to celebrating a heritage. At midnight on New Year's Eve, the year ends with a bang, and a new year begins with another holiday—New Year's Day. No wonder it's a time for family and friends to reach out to each other. Use the notes in this chapter to do just that.

Season's Greetings

You don't have to be religious to enjoy this time of year. A love of mistletoe, sleigh bells, and snow-covered landscapes is reason enough. Look to the following for inspiring notes to write.

To Family

Dear Mom and Dad,

At this season of the year, I can't help thinking about the wonderful memories I have of growing up: making angels in the snow, decorating the tree, sipping hot chocolate on a winter night. Have a beautiful holiday, and thanks for the memories.

Greeting Goofs

It's a mistake not to send someone a holiday card because he or she isn't religious. "Season's Greetings" and "Happy Holidays" cards work nicely—and don't forget to add a personal note.

We knew someday our family wouldn't all be together for the holidays, but it's still hard having you so far away. I'll miss your efficiency in the kitchen, your glowing face at the dinner table, and your exuberance unwrapping presents. I love you and miss you, Sis. Happy holidays.

To Friends and Co-Workers

Nothing can be more important this time of year than celebrating the people who bring joy to my life—my friends. May you enjoy a peaceful and happy holiday season, friend.

Working with you this year has been such a pleasure. I'd like to return the favor by wishing you much love, laughter, and joy during the holiday season and in the new year.

Inspirational

John Lennon once asked us to imagine everyone living in peace. It isn't hard to imagine at this time of year when every house is lit up—as if inviting the world to come in. What if the invitation could be with us all year? I wish you a peaceful holiday season and more.

The Write Way _____

A religious card may not be appropriate, but what's wrong with a little inspiration? Find a quote that expresses how you feel about this time of year and include it in your note.

Someone once said, "Perhaps the best Yuletide decoration is being wreathed in smiles." How true. The holidays bring out the smile—and the child—in us. Here's to keeping the holiday spirit all year round!

Hanukkah

Every year at this time, Jewish people gather to celebrate the Festival of Lights—Hanukkah. The 8-day holiday commemorates the restoring of religious freedom to the Jews more than 2,300 years ago and the miracle of the oil that kept the menorah burning for 8 days. Here are some words you can say to family and friends.

To Family

Dear Mom and Dad,

At Hanukkah, I always think how fortunate I am to have such dedicated parents. You kept our traditions alive when we were children, and now we pass them on to our own families. We are all part of a living history. We hope you have a joyful Hanukkah.

Wishing you a Hanukkah filled with gifts, fun, and plenty of good food. Especially food. Oy! You look like a bag of bones, son. Some latkes and rugelach will help fill you out a little. I'm kidding. You're perfect the way you are. Happy Hanukkah!

The Write Way _____

Mention some of the traditions of Hanukkah in your letter—lighting the menorah, eating latkes, gift giving, and gathering with family and friends.

To Friends and Co-Workers

Happy Hanukkah. This is a time of joy, love, and celebrating with our friends. We hope the miracle of light will fill your heart each day you light a new candle.

The Write Way _____

Don't forget to mention the holiday in your card. The beginning or end of a note is a good place to write it, but sometimes it fits nicely in the middle. Use your own judgment.

It's not often you can say a person you work with is a friend, but you are. We don't just share an office; we share our lives. Wishing my friend a Hanukkah full of joy, light, and peace.

Religious

I want to share a quote I came across once: "May love and light fill your home and heart at Hanukkah." And may the blessings of Hanukkah light your way throughout the year.

As we lovingly light the menorah candle each day of Hanukkah, let's ask God to light up our lives with his wisdom and love so that we, in turn, can light up the world. Happy Hanukkah.

Christmas

Christmas is a Christian holiday celebrating the birth of Jesus more than 2,000 years ago, but the world has adopted and expanded on its traditions. The first Christmas card was sent in 1843, and the rest is history. Add a special holiday greeting—like one of the following—to your note this year.

To Family

We're all ready for you. In the words of Clement Moore, "The stockings [are] hung by the chimney with care / In hopes that St. Nicholas soon [will] be there." I have one question for you—naughty or nice? Got you worried? See you at Christmas!

The Write Way

A little humor is okay at Christmas, as long as you know the person well and are sure he or she will enjoy it. There are plenty of Christmas traditions you can have fun with.

You probably know this, but I'm like a kid at Christmas. Is it the great food? The presents? The decorations? Singing Christmas carols? The children's pageant at church? Having my family all around? It's all that and more. Merry Christmas from the biggest kid in the family.

To Friends and Co-Workers

We wish you a merry Christmas, we wish you a merry Christmas, we wish you a merry Christmas and a happy New Year! Sorry, I'm just practicing my Christmas karaoke for the neighborhood open house. Or does "Silent Night" sound like a better idea? Whether they're silent or song-filled, let the Christmas celebrations begin!

It's "Secret Santa" time again at the office. I know the gift giver is supposed to remain anonymous, so I won't divulge my name. Well, maybe just a hint. Oh, what the heck. It's Matt in the next cube. Enjoy the Christmas stocking filled with chocolates—instead of raiding the stash in my desk drawer!

Religious

When you're opening the expensive presents and eating the rich food, remember where the true wealth of Christmas lies. As eighteenth-century clergyman Phillip Brooks said, "Christmas day is a day of joy and charity. May God make you very rich in both."

The Write Way _____

> Christmas is an excellent time to send a religious card. After all, it is a religious holiday, and many people expect it. Be thoughtful, still, of whether your card will be welcome.

Pope John XXIII said, "Mankind is a great, an immense family … This is proved by what we feel in our hearts at Christmas." Imagine what the world would be like if we kept the Christmas spirit all year round? God bless you at Christmas and every day of the year.

Kwanzaa

Based on the African "first fruits" festivals, Kwanzaa honors African American culture. Each night between Christmas and New Year's, a candle is lit to signal one of seven values: unity, self-determination, work and responsibility, cooperative economics, purpose, creativity, and faith. It's a good time to share with people the values you see in them.

To Family

When you were a boy, we taught you about your heritage so you could have a sense of pride and unity with your past. Now we watch you pass those lessons on to your children, and we realize that we are also united to our future. Past, present, and future have become one. Happy Kwanzaa.

The Write Way

Kwanzaa has been a holiday since 1966, but it's growing in popularity among African Americans. Focus on the seven values celebrated during the holiday and connect them to the person.

Martin Luther King Jr. had a dream, and he did something about it. You have a dream, too. May the spirit of Kwanzaa guide you to believing in yourself and making your dreams a reality.

To Friends and Co-Workers

In his poem "Mending Wall," Robert Frost said, "Good fences make good neighbors," but I disagree. Good neighbors work with you to make your home and neighborhood peaceful and inviting. Have a happy Kwanzaa, and thank you for being the best of neighbors.

You're such a creative businesswoman. The way you handle people at work—getting so much from them when they think they have nothing to give—is amazing. It's no wonder people respect you so much. Happy Kwanzaa. You represent the spirit of the holiday.

The Write Way

Kwanzaa is a great opportunity to compliment a co-worker. Let her know what you admire about her. Is she a leader, does she work hard, does she have a winning personality? Be specific.

Inspirational

Faith is a guiding principle of Kwanzaa—faith in your family, faith in your community, faith in yourself. Andrew Young took it one step further when he said, "My hope for my children must be that they respond to the still, small voice of God in their own hearts." May Kwanzaa unite our hearts in faith and unity.

Olympic medalist Jesse Owens once said, "The battles that count aren't the ones for gold medals. The struggles within yourself—the invisible, inevitable battles inside all of us—that's where it's at." As we celebrate Kwanzaa, I hope your struggles will lead you to excellence.

New Year's

"Hope springs eternal," said Alexander Pope, and it definitely does on New Year's Day. On this day we erase the past and start again with a clean slate. Here are a few words to inspire your friends and family to face the future with optimism.

To Family

New Year's Day—a great time to celebrate the memories we have of the people and places we love—and the new memories we have to look forward to. Happy New Year!

> **Greeting Goofs**
>
> Put the unhappy memories of the past behind you. A New Year's card can mention good memories but should focus on the future. Make your note optimistic and uplifting.

Losing weight, exercising, and keeping in better touch with family are popular New Year's resolutions. The first two sound like work, but the last one sounds like fun—especially with a great family like ours. Let's get together more this year, okay?

To Friends and Co-Workers

I just read that New Year's resolutions date to 153 B.C.E. I think it's time we broke with tradition, don't you? Starting this year, I promise to never make another resolution. Wait … that's a resolution, isn't it? Oh, forget it. Just have a happy new year!

The Write Way _____

A New Year's resolution is an excellent topic for your note—as long as you're not handing out advice. Write about your growing relationship and wish him or her a good year ahead.

Looking forward to new contracts, new clients, and a great new year working with you. Wishing you and your family the best in this holiday season and the new year.

Religious

A New Year's resolution shouldn't be made casually. You need to give it some thought, according to St. John Chrysostom. "When we once begin to form good resolutions," he wrote, "God gives us every opportunity of carrying them out." Choose wisely, and God will give you the strength to make it work. Happy New Year!

On New Year's Day, let's count the blessings God has given us. And may we be wise enough to recognize the blessings God gives us each day of the new year. Have a happy and holy year.

Inspirational

What is it about New Year's that makes everything seem possible? It's as if your soul has been washed clean of the past, and you have another chance to be a better person. Let's make it happen this time around. Have a new year that'll make you proud!

Why do we celebrate New Year's and its promises only one day of the year? Ralph Waldo Emerson said, "Write it on your heart that every day is the best day in the year." If we woke every morning with a feeling of hope in our hearts, imagine how wonderful life would be. Here's to a year full of happy New Year's days.

Quotes to Inspire You

Season's greetings quotes:

Blessed is the season which engages the whole world in a conspiracy of love. —*Hamilton Wright Mabie*

Yes, Virginia, there is a Santa Claus. He exists as certainly as love and generosity and devotion exists, and you know that they abound and give to your life its highest beauty and joy. —*Francis Pharcellus Church*

Christmas, my child, is love in action … Every time we love, every time we give, it's Christmas. —*Dale Evans Rogers*

Quotes about Hanukkah:

May the lights of Hanukkah usher in a better world for all humankind. —*Unknown*

Blessed is the match consumed in kindling flame / Blessed is the flame that burns in the secret fastness of the heart. —*Hannah Senesh*

To me every hour of the light and dark is a miracle / Every cubic inch of space is a miracle. —*Walt Whitman in* Leaves of Grass

Quotes about Christmas:

Christmas waves a magic wand over this world, and behold, everything is softer and more beautiful. —*Norman Vincent Peale*

Unless we make Christmas an occasion to share our blessings, all the snow in Alaska won't make it "white." —*Bing Crosby*

The only blind person at Christmastime is he who has not Christmas in his heart. —*Helen Keller*

Quotes about Kwanzaa:

Kwanzaa calls us also to recommit ourselves to our highest values. Cultural values that create and sustain the good world we all want and deserve to live in. —*Dr. Maulana Karenga, founder of Kwanzaa*

We all should know that diversity makes for a rich tapestry, and we must understand that all the threads of the tapestry are equal in value no matter what their color. —*Maya Angelou*

If you want to lift yourself up, lift up someone else. —*Booker T. Washington*

Quotes about New Year's:

Cheers to a new year and another chance for us to get it right. —*Oprah Winfrey*

Be always at war with your vices, at peace with your neighbors, and let each new year find you a better man. —*Benjamin Franklin*

Every new day begins with possibilities. It's up to us to fill it with things that move us toward progress and peace. —*Ronald Reagan*

Chapter 14

Honor Your Mother and Father

Mom and Dad—there's no one like them. They brought you into this world. Then they lovingly dressed you, fed you, and dried your tears until you could do the same for yourself. They also taught you how to stand, walk, run, jump, and—when the time was right—leap into your own life. They're the ones who always stand by you, no matter what the rest of the world says or does. No store-bought card can tell your parents exactly how you feel about them. But you can.

Mother's Day

Poets and songwriters have written pages about the beauty of a mother's love for her child. But none of their words can compare with the words that come from your own heart.

To Mothers

Thanks for always being there for me and for helping me believe in myself, Mom. It means a great deal that I can depend on you and that you always put me first. You're my inspiration. Happy Mother's Day from your son who loves you.

> **The Write Way**
>
> In your note, write about some of the things your mother has done for you and how much you appreciate it. The more personal and specific you are, the more she'll enjoy it.

Now that I'm a parent myself, I appreciate all the things you did for me growing up. Letting me win card games, hiking with me in the woods, cheering at Little League games and being quiet at golf matches, helping me apply to college, and trying not to cry when I left. I love you, Mom. Happy Mother's Day.

To Stepmothers

When you and Dad married, we didn't know, at first, how good you were for our family. You didn't force yourself on us but waited patiently for us to come to you. Thank you for that. I can say now that I've grown to love you, too. Have a happy Mother's Day.

Thank you for being so good to my father these last five years. You make each other happy, and that makes us "kids" happy, too. We're lucky to have you as our stepmother, and Dad's lucky to have you as his wife. Happy Mother's Day.

To Mothers-in-Law

When I married your son, I knew you'd be a wonderful mother-in-law. I had no idea you'd be my friend, too. The time we've spent together—whether shopping, cooking, or chatting on the phone—has been a delight. Happy Mother's Day, and thanks for being such a good friend.

Whoever writes those mother-in-law jokes obviously never met you, Mom. If they had, the jokes would be filled with compliments, not insults. You're a second mother to me, which means I get twice as much attention—and what man doesn't love that? Happy Mother's Day from your "other" son.

To Grandmothers

I remember looking forward to my summer visits with you when I was growing up. You made me feel a little bit spoiled with the great food, trips to the beach, and staying up late. Why don't we get together next weekend for a hug and some reminiscing? Happy Mother's Day to the best grandmother in the world.

Moms have to be the strict ones—telling kids to clean their rooms, do their homework, and stay out of trouble. But grandmas get to be the ones who spoil—playing endless games of Monopoly, baking the best cookies in the world, and doling out unlimited hugs and kisses. No one has ever spoiled me so well. Happy Mother's Day, Grandma!

To Daughters

As I watch you with your children, I feel so proud. You're affectionate, caring, patient, and strong. And you give them so much of yourself. You're exactly what a mother should be. Good job, sweetheart, and happy Mother's Day!

> **The Write Way** _____
>
> Let someone know how much she means to you and in what ways she is special to your life. There's no such thing as *too much* approval or gratitude.

I waited a long time to be a grandma, but the wait was worth it. You're a wonderful, loving, patient mother, and you're doing a fantastic job raising my beautiful grandchild. Of course, you had a good teacher— me! Seriously, I'm very proud of you, honey. Keep up the good work, and happy Mother's Day—every day.

To Stepdaughters

Although I didn't get to watch you grow up, your mother must have been amazing, because you're such a good mother yourself. I love the way you read to Rose and Sara every night before bed—I bet their dreams are filled with adventures. Happy Mother's Day to a wonderful stepdaughter.

I never had a daughter of my own, but you're as close to the real thing as they come. I'm lucky to have such a wonderful stepdaughter, and your boys are lucky to have such an exceptional mother. I love watching you do everything from play catch to bake cookies with them. Happy Mother's Day.

To Daughters-in-Law

Chris was a lucky man the day you agreed to marry him. Since then, you've made him even luckier. I don't know anyone I'd rather have as mother of my grandchildren. You're affectionate and patient, and you know how to have fun. What more could a child want? Wishing you a fun-filled Mother's Day.

The term "daughter-in-law" doesn't do you justice. "Second daughter" is so much nicer. So is "fantastic mother." I couldn't wish for a better mother for my grandchildren or a better wife for my son. Happy Mother's Day, second daughter.

Like a Mother

You're more than a friend; you're like a mother to me. No matter what happens, you're always there: guiding me, protecting me, and encouraging me. I don't know what I'd do without you in my life. Thank you for being a mother and a friend. Happy Mother's Day.

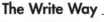
The Write Way

> If you have someone in your life—a friend, aunt, teacher, big sister—who's been like a mother to you, why not send her a card on Mother's Day? It's never too late to say thank you.

Children are lucky to have one loving mother, but I had two. Aunt Grace, you were a friend, confidant, and guiding light when I was growing up. Thank you for your open door, open ear, and open arm policy. Knowing you has enriched my life. Happy Mother's Day.

Mother's Day Blessings

Some people consider mothers gifts from God. What better day than Mother's Day to express that?

Religious

You're such an amazing mother. Whenever I'm in trouble, you seem to be right there. And you always know the right thing to say or do. It reminds me of a Jewish proverb I read once: "God could not be everywhere and therefore he made mothers." I'm so glad he made you for me. Have a blessed Mother's Day.

William Makepeace Thackeray said, "Mother is the name for God in the lips and hearts of little children." When I was a child, your love meant everything. Now I see the same expectations in my own children. Maybe it's how we get to know what God's love is like, through our mothers. I hope you feel God's love on Mother's Day.

Spiritual

"Mother: the most beautiful word on the lips of mankind." Kahlil Gibran wrote that, and I couldn't agree more. You're my support, my encouragement, my inspiration. No matter what I do, you never stop loving me. There is no greater gift. Happy Mother's Day to my beautiful mother.

I love this quote: "To the world, you might just be one person, but to one person, you might just be the world." You're the world to me, Mom. You always have been. I can't imagine going through life without your love and support. Happy Mother's Day.

The Write Way _____

Sometimes a quote says it better than you can. Don't hesitate to use one for inspiration—and then add a few words of your own.

Father's Day

Whether he's strong and silent or walks around with his heart wide open, what father doesn't want to know he's appreciated? A few kind words are all it takes.

To Fathers

You weren't the emotional type, Dad, but beneath your tough exterior, you loved us dearly. You taught us how to stand on our own feet, you helped us explore the world, and you always managed to be there when we needed you. Happy Father's Day to a dad who showed his love when it counted.

Greeting Goofs _____

Avoid flowery language when you write a Father's Day note. Most men don't appreciate it. Just say what you feel in a simple and straightforward way.

Author Barbara Johnson said, "To be in your children's memories tomorrow, you have to be in their lives today." You've always been involved in our lives, Dad, and you still are. Thanks for the wonderful childhood memories, and for all the memories to come. Happy Father's Day.

To Stepfathers

When you first joined our family, you had some pretty big shoes to fill. My dad was quite a man when he was alive. Looking back, I don't think we could have found a better fit. Happy Father's Day to a great guy.

Being a stepfather can't be easy. I can only imagine the apprehension you felt being "new dad on the block" in our family. I hope we weren't too hard on you in the beginning, but we only wanted the best for our mom. Turns out, that's what we got. Happy Father's Day to the best stepdad on the block.

To Fathers-in-Law

I might not call you Dad, but I can't tell you how often I think of you that way. You remind me of your son—loving, dependable, ready to help anyone in trouble. Happy Father's Day, and thanks for passing on the good genes! We love you.

When you first asked me to call you "Dad," I was hesitant. I already have a dad …. But then I got to know you and love you, and calling you "Dad" came naturally. Happy Father's Day, Dad, and thank you for welcoming me into your family.

To Grandfathers

Someone once said, "A grandfather is someone with silver in his hair and gold in his heart." Yup. There's definitely silver in the little bit of hair you have left, Grandpa. But the vein of gold in your heart is so deep it can never run out. Wishing you a happy Father's Day.

Here's a quote from a writer named Louis Adamic that reminds me of you: "My grandfather always said that living is like licking honey off a thorn." Your life hasn't been easy, Gramps, but you always saw the good in it. I'd like to do that in my life, too. Happy Father's Day, and thanks for the lesson.

To Sons

I'm so proud of the wonderful father you are. You and Sue are so creative with Jacque. You read to her, sing songs, and encourage her to use her imagination, and it's already had a positive effect. She's a delightful and creative little girl, thanks to you. Happy Father's Day, and keep up the good work!

The Write Way

Write a card to your own children who are mothers or fathers. Be specific about how they parent, and let them know you're proud. They never stop needing your approval, no matter how old they get.

Here's a quote that hits home: "We never know the love of our parents for us till we have become parents." Henry Ward Beecher, a nineteenth-century clergyman, said that, but he could've been talking about me. Son, my love for you has been steadfast since the moment I first laid eyes on you, and I hope now that you're a father yourself, you'll under-stand just how deep my love is for you. Happy Father's Day.

To Stepsons

We've had our moments—I guess that's part of growing up—but I want you to know how much I care for you. Although we don't always think alike, I respect your enthusiasm and ability to stand up for your own ideas. You're also an excellent father and husband. Wishing you a Father's Day filled with joy.

Greeting Goofs

You might not always agree with someone, but arguments don't belong in Father's Day cards. Be honest about your relationship, but find something positive to say, too.

Thinking back, I realize our relationship hasn't always been smooth sailing. We had some major disagreements, but I think we worked them out pretty well—sometimes with your mother's help! I know she's proud to call you "Son" ... and so am I. Have a great Father's Day.

To Sons-in-Law

It's not easy for a father to hand over his daughter to another man, but you've proved yourself worthy of her love. And you must be doing something right as a father, because your kids are crazy about you. So I guess it's time for me to say, "Happy Father's Day, Son. You're doing okay."

Happy Father's Day, Adam. You're a great husband to our daughter, a devoted father to our grandchildren, and an all-around good guy. You deserve a day to rest and relax, and so does Pam. How about we come over Sunday after church to babysit? See you then!

Like a Father

I never told you this, but you're a great guy. You take me on cool trips, like my dad would if he was around. I liked fishing and playing basketball. I really liked the time we went to see the Nets play. I can't send my dad a card, so I'm sending one to you because you're like a dad to me sometimes. Happy Father's Day.

I'm afraid this Father's Day card is long overdue. When I was growing up, you were like a second father to me. I remember how we all piled into your station wagon to go camping and to ball games or movies. You treated me like one of your own, and I'll never forget it. Happy Father's Day to a great guy.

Father's Day Blessings

"Blessed indeed is the man who hears many gentle voices call him father!" wrote Lydia M. Child. If your father likes the idea of being blessed, why not let him know how much he is?

Religious

On this Father's Day, Dad, I wanted to share a quote from the Talmud: "When you teach your son, you teach your son's son." Thanks for being such a good teacher, Dad. Now that I'm a father, I plan to pass on what you taught me to my own son. Happy Father's Day to both of us.

I always thought God was a little like you, Dad. You love me unconditionally—and that's how I know what it's like to be loved by God. William Wordsworth said it best: "Father!—to God himself we cannot give a holier name." Happy Father's Day.

 The Write Way

Tell your parents what you've learned from them and how it affects your life. Let them know you're teaching those lessons to your own kids.

Spiritual

Homer wrote, "It is a wise child that knows his own father." It took a while, but now that I'm a father, I'm a little wiser and I understand you much better. The love, the concern, the need to protect—it's all part of who a father is. Thank you for being a great dad. Happy Father's Day.

I read this recently: "A man's children and his garden both reflect the amount of weeding done during the growing season." Just wanted to thank you, Dad, for paying attention when I was growing up and not letting me go wild. Happy Father's Day to a dad who cared enough to put his foot down.

Quotes to Inspire You

Quotes about Mother's Day:

A mother is a person who, seeing there are only four pieces of pie for five people, promptly announces she never did care for pie. —*Unknown*

There is only one pretty child in the world, and every mother has it. —*Chinese proverb*

To describe my mother would be to write about a hurricane in its perfect power. —*Maya Angelou*

The doctors told me I would never walk, but my mother told me I would, so I believed my mother. —*Wilma Rudolph*

Mama exhorted her children at every opportunity to "jump at de sun." We might not land on the sun, but at least we would get off the ground. —*Zora Neale Hurston*

Quotes about Father's Day:

It is not flesh and blood but the heart which makes us fathers and sons. —*Johann Schiller*

Fatherhood is pretending the present you love most is soap-on-a-rope. —*Bill Cosby*

My dad has always taught me these words: *care* and *share*. That's why we put on clinics. The only thing I can do is try to give back. —*Tiger Woods*

My father didn't tell me how to live; he lived, and let me watch him do it. —*Clarence B. Kelland*

My father gave me the greatest gift anyone could give another person, he believed in me. —*Jim Valvano*

Chapter 15

Other Holidays

Thanks to Hallmark, the U.S. government, and the world's most popular religions, there's at least one holiday for each of the 365 days of the year, covering all areas from religion to patriotism, from romance to just plain fun. Not every holiday calls for a card or even a note, but a few are good candidates. If one of these holidays touches your heart, your soul, or your imagination, share your thoughts with a note.

All About God

Whether you're Christian, Jewish, Muslim, or Hindu, you'll have more than one opportunity to celebrate your religious heritage. With a medley of Irish blessings and quotes from the Bible and the Koran, here are some notes to inspire you.

St. Patrick's Day

There are so many beautiful Irish blessings, and I wanted to find the perfect one to express my wish for you today. Here it is: "May St. Patrick guard you wherever you go, and guide you in whatever you do—and may his loving protection be a blessing to you always." Happy St. Patrick's Day.

I just wanted to wish an old friend an old Irish blessing on his favorite holiday. "May the Good Lord take a liking to you … but not too soon!" We have a lot of good years of friendship ahead of us. Have a happy and blessed St. Patrick's Day.

Easter

On this holy day, I thank God for bringing the hope of new life to us. As Ralph Waldo Emerson said, "He takes men out of time and makes them feel eternity." I wish you peace, love, and a fresh start this Easter.

Wishing you great joy this time of year. May Easter and the return of spring give your life new meaning so you can pursue your hopes and dreams with God by your side.

Passover

I think of you at Passover, sharing the Seder and celebrating our history. I pray that you'll have a joyful Passover and that its blessings will remain with you throughout the year. Shalom.

Greeting Goofs

Don't write a note to someone of a different faith without doing your homework. A little Internet research helps you say something specific about the holiday your friends are celebrating.

It's Passover again. Time to celebrate our freedom, a precious gift we must safeguard because we've lost it so many times in our history. As the Danish proverb says, "Better to be a free bird than a captive king." Happy Passover.

Ramadan

It's a difficult time in the history of the world, but these words translated from the Koran can teach us how to live: "If they seek peace, then seek you peace. And trust in God for He is the One that heareth and knoweth all things." (8:61) May you enjoy a peaceful and blessed Ramadan.

The Write Way

Ramadan is a month-long fast—a time of prayer to Allah (God) and contemplation of the Koran. It ends at Eid al-Fitr, a day of rejoicing, as family and friends gather to pray and exchange gifts. A common greeting for any Islamic holiday is *Eid Mubarak,* which means "have a blessed Holiday."

I hope all your prayers were answered this month of the Koran. May the blessings of Allah fill your life with peace and love. Eid Mubarak to you and your family.

Jewish New Year

As we keep the High Holy Days, we reflected on the past year and hope to make the next one better. One way to do this is to spend more time with friends like you. L'Shanah Tovah.

The Write Way

The Jewish New Year begins with Rosh Hashanah and ends with Yom Kippur. Here are a couple Hebrew expressions you can use in your notes: *L'Shanah Tovah* means "for a good year," and *Shalom* means "peace," "well-being," or simply "hello."

L'Shanah Tovah. We look forward to being with you on Rosh Hashanah and sharing our holiday meal. We hope the new year brings us no sorrow, but much peace and happiness.

Diwali

Can't wait for Diwali to begin. It's so much fun to dress up in new clothes, nibble on sweets, and light firecrackers. Most of all, I enjoy spending the holiday with you because "you light up my life." Happy Diwali!

The Write Way

Diwali is a joyous Hindu new year celebration that lasts five days. The third and main day is the Festival of Lights. People light candles and diyas (lamps) at home, burst firecrackers at night, and come together to feast and exchange gifts—all to symbolize the victory of light (knowledge) over darkness (ignorance).

As we celebrate the Festival of Lights, I wish you a new year that is happy, wise, and prosperous. May your home glow with the light of friendship and peace. Have a bright and happy Diwali.

All About Tributes

Don't you love parades and flag-waving and all that patriotic fun? It means a lot to some people that you appreciate their sacrifices for our country. Why not celebrate the earth, too, while you're at it? Here's how.

Martin Luther King Day

Martin Luther King Jr. said, "Life's most persistent and urgent question is, 'What are you doing for others?'" That's a question you've answered. No one volunteers as much as you do. On his day, maybe it's time I joined you. What a perfect way to celebrate the day, the man, and the dream. "Let freedom ring!"

I know how much this day means to you, because freedom is not something we should ever take for granted. King said, "Darkness cannot drive out darkness; only light can do that. Hate cannot drive out hate; only love can do that." Let's carry the banner of light and love for his sake and ours. Happy MLK Day!

Earth Day

I know how much you love nature so I wanted to share this quote with you: "And this, our life … finds tongues in trees, books in the running brooks, sermons in stones, and good in everything." Can you believe William Shakespeare wrote that 400 years ago? Happy Earth Day.

The Write Way

Celebrate the earth? Why not? You're honoring the people who work so hard to be good caretakers of our planet.

Did you know that Earth Day was first celebrated on April 22, 1970, and that today, 140 nations observe it? I looked that up, hoping to impress you like you impress me with your dedication to saving energy and preserving the environment. Happy Earth Day to my favorite tree hugger.

Memorial Day

I know this is a difficult day for you. You lost a father and a son in two wars. Writer/songwriter Randy Vader said, "The story of America's quest for freedom is inscribed on her history in the blood of her patriots." It's important that we acknowledge the sacrifice they—and you—made for us all on this Memorial Day.

Greeting Goofs

American holidays are all about resting and having fun. But don't forget the real meaning of Memorial Day (honoring the dead) and Veterans Day (honoring the living veterans). Servicemen and servicewomen and their families will appreciate a note from you.

Wow! Summer's here and we have three days off from work. It's Memorial Day! With all the parades and barbecues, it's easy to forget the real meaning of this holiday: remembering the soldiers who gave their lives for this country. You had friends who died in Vietnam, and I've lost friends in Iraq. Let's remember them together.

The Fourth of July

Daniel Webster said, "May the sun in his course visit no land more free, more happy, more lovely, than this our own country!" So heat up your grills and lay on those dogs. Time to celebrate the ol' red, white, and blue. Happy birthday to the USA!

The Fourth of July is the day we celebrate our freedom with fireworks and flag-waving, parades and picnics. If I could send a card to our great country, I'd write, "I'm proud to be an American!" I can't, so I'm sending a card to you, the most patriotic person I know. Happy Fourth of July!

Veterans Day

On Veterans Day, thank you for all you've done for our country. John F. Kennedy reminded us, "As we express our gratitude, we must never forget that the highest appreciation is not to utter words, but to live by them." I hope our actions do justice to you and our men and women who fight for freedom in the world.

Veterans Day is when we honor our servicemen and servicewomen for all the sacrifices they've made for our freedom. You bravely fought in Iraq for two tours of duty, and I'm profoundly grateful. Thank you today, November 11, and every day of the year. You're my hero.

All About Tradition

Tradition is another reason to celebrate a holiday. Thanksgiving has been popular since the Pilgrims first observed it. Chinese and Mexican immigrants brought their own traditions to our country, too—all reasons to celebrate!

Chinese New Year

Whether you were born in the year of the Pig, Monkey, Rat, or some other animal, happy New Year and happy birthday. And don't forget to clean your house and turn over a new leaf. I have a feeling an abundance of wealth will be coming your way. How do I know? A little red envelope tells me so.

The Write Way

Chinese New Year is a 15-day celebration, honoring one of the 12 animals in the Chinese zodiac each year. People wear red, visit family, pray to gods and ancestors, eat foods for good fortune, and give "lucky money" to children in red envelopes. Houses are cleaned and firecrackers are lit to ward off evil spirits.

Wishing you harmony and good fortune this year. May your days be filled with happiness, prosperity, and moments you'll always remember. Happy New Year!

Cinco de Mayo

Emily Dickinson said long ago, "A LITTLE madness in the Spring / Is wholesome even for the King ..." She probably wasn't thinking about Cinco de Mayo, but why not? Let's enjoy our crazy holiday with carnivals, parades, food, and plenty of margaritas. Have a happy Cinco de Mayo!

> **The Write Way** _____
>
> Cinco de Mayo (the Fifth of May) is a holiday observed by many Mexican Americans as a celebration of Mexican pride, culture, and heritage. Other Americans enjoy the holiday with its emphasis on Mexican food, drink, music, and parades.

Some people call Cinco de Mayo the Mexican St. Patrick's Day because there's so much partying. But that's where the resemblance ends. Forget just green—throw in some white and red, too! Forget beer—break out the tequila! Forget … oh, forget it! Let's just celebrate spring with a joyous Cinco de Mayo!

Thanksgiving

"If the only prayer you said in your whole life was 'thank you,' that would suffice." German theologian Meister Eckhart said that back in the twelfth century, but the words mean just as much today. Have a wonderful, warm Thanksgiving with your family.

In the nineteenth century, author and preacher E. P. Powell said, "Thanksgiving Day is a jewel, to set in the hearts of honest men; but be careful that you do not take the day, and leave out the gratitude." I'm grateful every day for my big, boisterous, loving family. I can't wait for Thanksgiving dinner!

All About Fun

Some holidays are all about having a good time. Even a few religious holidays like Easter and St. Patrick's Day have a playful side to them. Keep reading for clues about what to write.

> **Greeting Goofs** _____
>
> When sending a St. Patrick's Day note, be different and don't make alcohol-related jokes. Concentrate on the parades, silly green hats, and other fun aspects of the holiday instead.

St. Patrick's Day

If you're lookin' for a little bit o' blarney, how about a four-leaf clover, green beer, little men in funny hats, and pots of gold at the end of a rainbow. Happy St. Patrick's Day!

Someone once said, "There are only two kinds of people in the world, the Irish and those who wish they were." Maybe that's why we celebrate St. Patrick's Day with such wild abandon, so people who aren't Irish can pretend they are, and people who are Irish can be grateful they are. Happy St. Patrick's Day!

Easter

When Easter comes around, we're inundated with jelly beans and baskets of colored eggs. "All I really need is love" said Lucy in Charles Schulz's comic strip *Peanuts*, "but a little chocolate now and then doesn't hurt!" Here's hoping you get a chocolate bunny for Easter.

Even when we were kids, we knew rabbits didn't lay Easter eggs, but we still loved getting Easter baskets filled with jelly beans, foil-covered chocolate eggs, and best of all, those big hollow chocolate bunnies. I hope this Easter basket brings back sweet childhood memories.

Halloween

If you're worried about "things that go bump in the night," then this isn't the holiday for you. But I know you like dressing up like someone (or something) you couldn't be in a million years—and you're not afraid of the dark (and love candy)—so you've hit the jackpot! Happy Halloween.

I love this quote by humor writer Erma Bombeck: "A grandmother pretends she doesn't know who you are on Halloween." Frankly, I think people of all ages should dress up on Halloween and pretend they don't recognize each other. I'm up for a costume party, are you? Let's plan it together.

All About Love

According to Hallmark, about 187 million Valentine's Day cards are sold every year, making it the second most popular holiday for sending cards. With so many cards exchanging hands, people can end up getting the same card twice. Let's hope that doesn't happen to you, but if it does, your handwritten note can save the day by making the card personal and meaningful.

Valentines to Family

French poet and philosopher Paul Valéry must've been talking about our family when he said, "Love is being stupid together." How lucky we are to have a dominant gene for silliness in our family! I love you, Mom and Dad. Happy Valentine's Day, and thanks for making growing up so much fun.

The Write Way

Valentine's Day isn't just for lovers. Send cards to your family and friends, too. And the children you know. Tell everyone how much you love them.

I'm sending you a valentine this year. Why? Ever since we were kids, I could always count on you. That's just who you are. So today I want to tell you how much I love you—for being the best sister and friend anyone could have. Happy Valentine's Day.

Valentines to Friends

I thought of you two when I read this quote from writer Armistead Maupin: "Like I've always said, love wouldn't be blind if the Braille weren't so damned much fun." Happy Valentine's Day to two people who can't keep their hands off each other, even after being married 20 years!

I'm spreading the love this year, so all my friends are getting a card and lots of hugs and kisses for being so supportive. Did I mention the kisses were chocolate? Happy Valentine's Day!

Valentines to Loved Ones

That incurable romantic Albert Einstein once said, "Gravitation is not responsible for people falling in love." Nonsense! When I first saw you, I was irresistibly pulled in your direction and I fell hard. I'm still falling— in love, that is. Happy Valentine's Day to the object of my attraction.

Love is in the air—just as it always is when you're around. I'm not good with words, but after 12 years together, I need to tell you something. You are my love and my life. Happy Valentine's Day.

Valentines to Children

Someone once wrote, "A hundred hearts would be too few to carry all my love for you." I could draw 100 hearts on this card, but it still wouldn't show how much love I have in my real heart for you. Happy Valentine's Day, grandson.

I have a box of hearts for you. Each one has a special message from me. You can read them. Guess what? You can eat them, too. Will you be my valentine?

Quotes to Inspire You

Quotes about God:

May the strength of God pilot us, may the wisdom of God instruct us, may the hand of God protect us, may the word of God direct us. Be always ours this day and for evermore. —*St. Patrick*

Our Lord has written the promise of the resurrection, not in books alone, but in every leaf in spring-time. —*Martin Luther*

A good word is like a good tree whose root is firmly fixed and whose top is in the sky. —*translated from the Koran*

Quotes about tributes:

I have a dream that my four little children will one day live in a nation where they will not be judged by the color of their skin, but by the content of their character. —*Martin Luther King Jr.*

A hero is someone who has given his or her life to something bigger than oneself. —*Joseph Campbell*

There are no passengers on Spaceship Earth. We are all crew. —*Marshall McLuhan*

Quotes about tradition:

To attract good fortune, spend a new coin on an old friend, share an old pleasure with a new friend, and lift up the heart of a true friend by writing his name on the wings of a dragon. —*Chinese proverb*

What potent blood hath modest May. —*Ralph Waldo Emerson*

As we express our gratitude, we must never forget that the highest appreciation is not to utter words, but to live by them. —*John Fitzgerald Kennedy*

Quotes about fun:

Never iron a four-leaf clover because you don't want to press your luck. —*Unknown*

Don't put all your eggs in one basket. —*Unknown*

Nothing on Earth so beautiful as the final haul on Halloween night. —*Steve Almond*

Quotes about love:

The Eskimos had fifty-two names for snow because it was important to them: there ought to be as many for love. —*Margaret Atwood*

Real love stories never have endings. —*Richard Bach*

Appendix A

E-Mail Do's and Don'ts

In today's fast-paced world, handwriting and mailing notes isn't always practical. Luckily there's an alternative: e-mail. E-mails are appropriate in some situations and absolutely wrong in others. And even when they're appropriate, you can goof. Who hasn't dashed off a note, clicked the Send button, and then had that sinking feeling in the pit of his or her stomach? Use the following tips to help prevent that feeling so you can send more effective e-mail messages.

Don't …

◆ Use e-mail to send birthday greetings, anniversary wishes, or wishes for any other important occasion. It shouts, "I just don't care that much!" The same goes for e-cards, which tell the recipient, "I forgot until the last minute."

◆ Send condolences via e-mail. Ever.

◆ Make recipients decipher a message filled with misspellings and typos. On the other hand, don't correct anyone else's spelling. That's rude. Check your grammar and spelling with the spellchecker before hitting Send.

◆ Send back the whole message if you're just replying, "Okay." When a message thread gets long, delete all but the last e-mail.

◆ Type *Urgent* in the subject line if a message isn't. People might start treating you like the boy who cried wolf.

◆ Use vague phrases in your subject lines, like "Response to your e-mail." Be specific, or the recipient might think it's spam and delete it.

◆ Type in UPPERCASE letters. This is "shouting" in e-mail parlance and is rude.

◆ Use colorful fonts.

◆ Use a lot of exclamation marks.

◆ Use emoticons unless you want to sound like a 10-year-old.

◆ Send an angry e-mail without waiting until you've calmed down some.

◆ Forward a friend's e-mail to anyone else without his permission. If he wrote you a letter, you wouldn't copy it and send it to someone else, would you?

◆ Forward chain letters. If you find chain letters, jokes, and other such e-mails annoying, ask people to please stop sending them to you.

Greeting Goofs

Handwriting an angry letter and taking it to the post office can take hours, and by that time, you might cool off and decide not to send it. Zinging off an angry e-mail takes only a few minutes—but the repercussions can last a long time, maybe even forever. Wait an hour or a day before sending the e-mail. You may have a whole different perspective by then.

Do ...

◆ Use e-mail to keep in touch with out-of-town friends and send quick messages to local friends.

◆ Use e-mail to say thanks for a small favor; for example, if some-one recommends a restaurant to you.

◆ Use e-mail to keep in touch with people who are housebound or chronically ill or to offer encouragement to someone having surgery shortly.

◆ Use e-mail to reinforce or follow up a phone call or note in the mail.

◆ Use e-mail to offer long-term encouragement to out-of-town friends; for example, if they're job hunting.

◆ Express yourself clearly, so your message won't be misinterpreted.

◆ When receiving an e-mail, reread it to be sure you understand its meaning.

◆ Check and double check before sending an e-mail that says something personal about a third party, and be absolutely sure no one else will receive the message. For example, you might receive an e-mail from one person and then decide to comment on that e-mail to a third person. Instead of hitting Forward, you hit Reply. Oops. Your e-mail just went back to the sender.

◆ Dash off a quick (but grammatical) response saying you'll write again in a few days if you don't have time to answer an e-mail immediately. Then keep your promise.

◆ Reread e-mails you receive to be sure you understand their meaning.

Greeting Goofs

E-mail is especially prone to being misunderstood, because it's usually dashed off quickly. Taking an extra 30 seconds to rewrite an ambiguous phrase is easier than trying to explain what you meant later on.

Appendix B

Resources

This appendix includes sources of information on note writing, correct grammar usage, and inspirational quotes on a variety of subjects.

Note Writing

If you still find yourself searching for the right words, the following books and websites should give you even more advice on writing the best notes you can.

Daniel, J. Beverly. *Finding the Right Words: Perfect Phrases to Personalize Your Greeting Cards.* New York: Pocket Books, 2003.

Isaacs, Florence. *Just a Note to Say ...: The Perfect Words for Every Occasion.* New York: Clarkson Potter/Publishers, 2005.

Lamb, Sandra E. *Personal Notes: How to Write from the Heart for Any Occasion.* New York: St. Martin's Press, 2003.

Maggio, Rosalie. *How to Say It: Choice Words, Phrases, Sentences, and Paragraphs for Every Situation, Revised Edition.* New York: Prentice Hall, 2001.

About.Com
http://dying.about.com/od/lossgrief/a/console_letter.htm
Check here for step-by-step guidelines for a condolence letter.

American Hospice Foundation
www.americanhospice.org/griefzone/articles/condolence.htm
This site offers good advice about the do's and don'ts of writing
condolence notes.

Brownielocks and The 3 Bears
www.brownielocks.com/notes.html
Find tips for writing notes for various occasions, such as birthdays,
anniversaries, new babies/adoptions, holidays, rites of passage,
thank yous, get well, sympathy, and condolence. Sample letters are
included.

EAssortment
http://mtmt.essortment.com/howtowritetha_ruqo.htm
Guidelines for how to write a thank you card are presented here.

eHow
www.ehow.com/information_1058-etiquette.html
This page offers links to articles on letter writing, invitations
and RSVPs, correspondence, thank you notes, and gift-giving
etiquette.

Hallmark Pressroom
http://pressroom.hallmark.com
Check here for information about holidays and other card-buying
occasions.

Perfect Wording Ideas
www.perfect-wording-ideas.com
This site gives you ideas and sample letters for birthday invitations and thank yous, baby showers, wedding announcements and
replies, and more.

Wendy's World
www.wendy.com/letterwriting
Wendy offers letter-writing information, including Technique and Construction sections that cover writing love letters and condolence letters as well as cursive writing and letter-writing rules.

WritingHelp-Central
www.writinghelp-central.com/sample-letters-personal.html
Find sample personal letters of different types at this page.

Quotations

When you want the perfect quote to accompany your note—or give you inspiration to get started—check these sources:

Bartlett, John. *Bartlett's Familiar Quotations: A Collection of Passages, Phrases, and Proverbs Traced to Their Sources in Ancient and Modern Literature* (17th Edition). Boston: Little, Brown and Company, 2002.

Documents and Designs
www.documentsanddesigns.com/wedding_vows.htm
Check here for quotes about marriage, weddings, and love.

Birthday Messages
www.birthdaymessages.com
This site is exactly what it says—lists of short birthday messages to include in cards—from funny to inspirational.

Famous Quotes and Quotations.com
www.famous-quotes-and-quotations.com/love-quotes.html
This site offers top 10 quotes in different categories.

The Quote Garden
www.quotegarden.com
Here, quotes are alphabetized by topic, holidays and special occasions, hot topics, and sayings for teens.

Thinkexist.com
www.thinkexist.com
Log on here and search quotes by author, topic, keyword, and more.

Useful Information
www.useful-information.info/index.html
This site has a "Famous Quotes" index with quotes on family, love, relationships, inspiration, holidays, humor, and more.

World of Quotes.com
www.worldofquotes.com
Alphabetically browse quotes by topic and proverbs by ethnicity here.

Grammar

Grammar—you either love it or hate it. Go to the following sources to be sure you get it right!

Manhard, Stephen J. *The Goof-Proofer: How to Avoid the 41 Most Embarrassing Errors in Your Speaking and Writing*. New York: Fireside, 1998.

Strunk Jr., William, and E. B. White. *The Elements of Style, Fourth Edition*. New York: Longman, 2000.

Index

T

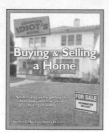

Great gifts for *any* occasion!

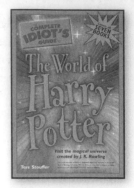